THE CATHOLIC UNIVERSITY OF AMERICA
CANON LAW STUDIES
No. 250

THE FUNCTIONS RESERVED TO PASTORS

A Historical Synopsis and a Commentary

BY

REVEREND BERNARD M. KELLY, S.T.L., J.C.L.
PRIEST OF THE DIOCESE OF PROVIDENCE

A DISSERTATION

SUBMITTED TO THE FACULTY OF THE SCHOOL OF CANON LAW OF THE CATHOLIC UNIVERSITY OF AMERICA IN PARTIAL FULFILLMENT OF THE REQUIREMENTS FOR THE DEGREE OF DOCTOR OF CANON LAW

THE CATHOLIC UNIVERSITY OF AMERICA PRESS
WASHINGTON, D. C.
1947

Nihil Obstat:
CLEMENS V. BASTNAGEL, J.U.D., S.T.L.
Censor Deputatus
Washingtonii, D. C., die 27 maii, 1947.

Imprimatur:
✠ FRANCISCUS P. KEOUGH, D.D.,
Episcopus Providentiensis
Providentiae, R. I., die 29 maii, 1947.

MURRAY & HEISTER—WASHINGTON, D. C.
PRINTED IN THE UNITED STATES OF AMERICA

9

To

MARY QUEEN OF THE CLERGY

TABLE OF CONTENTS

PART ONE—HISTORICAL SYNOPSIS

CHAPTER I

CHAPTER II

PART TWO—CANONICAL COMMENTARY

CHAPTER III

CHAPTER IV

CHAPTER V

CHAPTER VI

FOREWORD

It will be the purpose of this dissertation to examine in detail certain exclusive prerogatives which have been accorded by law to pastors in connection with their parochial office. Most of the reserved parochial functions have already received extensive study, as canonical institutions, in the writings of contemporary canonists. As functions whose exercise is reserved to pastors, however, they have been given but slight consideration. This defect the writer has undertaken to supply in some substantial, although imperfect manner.

Although it is true that the reserved parochial functions connote an obligation as well as a right, they will receive consideration in this dissertation solely from the aspect of parochial rights. An effort will be made to determine their nature, juridic force and legal implications from the honorary viewpoint only.

The writer takes this occasion to express his sincere gratitude to the Most Reverend Francis P. Keough, D.D., Bishop of Providence, for the opportunity to pursue advanced studies in Canon Law; to the Faculty of the School of Canon Law at the Catholic University of America, Washington, D. C., for their kind guidance and assistance; and to all others who have aided in any way in the preparation of this work.

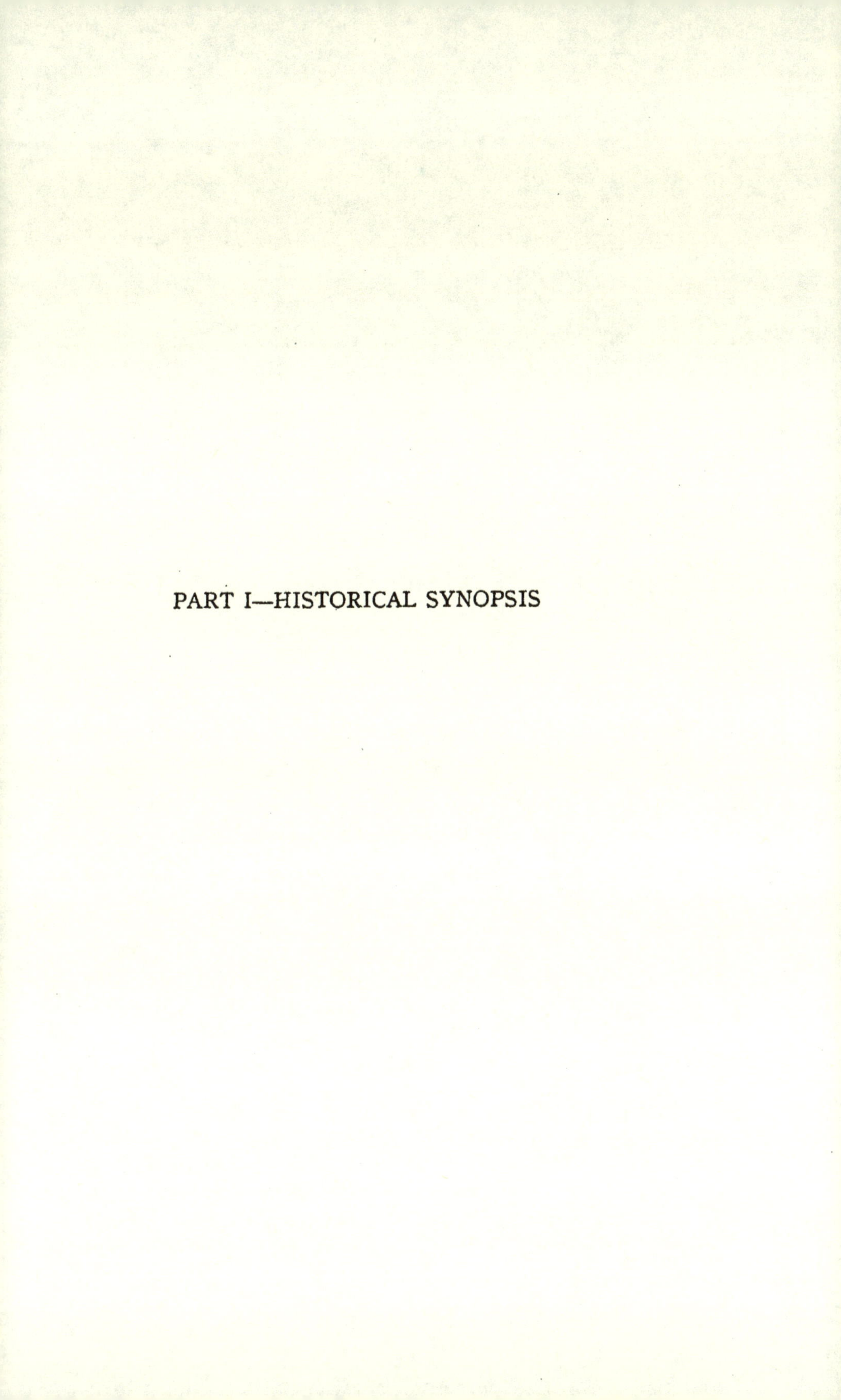

PART I—HISTORICAL SYNOPSIS

CHAPTER I

THE DEVELOPMENT OF PAROCHIAL RIGHTS BEFORE THE COUNCIL OF TRENT (1545–1563)

ARTICLE 1. *The Origin of Parishes*

THE most characteristic feature of the Church in antiquity was the centralization of all ecclesiastical jurisdiction in the hands of the bishop. One looks in vain for any trace of a complex hierarchical structure, like the one, for example, that is characteristic of the Church today. All power was reserved to the bishop directly, to be exercised at his discretion personally or through those to whom he committed it. He alone could administer the sacraments. He alone in his own right offered the Divine Sacrifice. He and only he had the power to administer the temporal goods of the Church. The activity of priests and deacons depended completely on the will of the bishop.[1]

With the growth of the Church, however, the bishop found it necessary to appoint certain districts of his diocese to the care of his clerics, giving them the power to perform the more common spiritual functions for the benefit of the faithful residing in that district. It is difficult to determine just when this first de-centralization of diocesan jurisdiction occurred. The *Liber Pontificalis* credits Pope Dionysius (259–268) with first establishing the *Tituli* as parishes in Rome.[2] But it was not until the fourth century that the title churches actually functioned as parishes. It was only then that fixed residences were supplied for the clergy attached to them, thus distinguishing them from the other churches of Rome which did not furnish permanent residence for the clergy.[3]

---

[1] St. Ignatius, *Ep. ad Smyrnas,* cap. 8, 1: ". . . . non licet sine episcopo neque baptizare neque agapen celebrare."—Migne, *Patrologiae Cursus Completus, Series Graeca* (161 vols., Parisiis, 1856–1866), V, 714.

[2] Cf. Duchesne, *Le Liber Pontificalis, Texte, Introduction et Commentaire* (2 vols., Paris, 1886–1892), I, 157.

[3] J. Christ, "The Origin and Development of the term 'Tituli,'" *The Jurist,* IV, (1944), 101–123.

The development in Rome, however, was unique. It seems safe to say that the first definite sign of parochial organization in the West appears in the legislation of the Council of Elvira (ca. 305).[4] For at about this time there appeared among the chapels and oratories that dotted the Gallic and Spanish countryside a more permanent parochial institution called the "*ecclesia baptismalis*" or "*ecclesia major.*" [5] Here for the first time there was established a stable, juridic relationship between the faithful in a definite locality and one individual church that was presided over by a priest.[6]

Moreover, certain rights were exclusively assigned to the pastor with respect to the people entrusted to his care. This is evident from the famous pseudo-Isidorian decretal, a reputed instruction of Pope Dionysius to Severus, bishop of Cordova in Spain, in which the Sovereign Pontiff stated that he had divided the parishes and cemeteries among the priests and had clearly defined their respective rights, so that no one might infringe upon the limits of another parish, but rather be content to function within his own boundaries, for the benefit of the flock entrusted to his care.[7] The fact that this decretal is reproduced in many canonical collections of the Middle Ages testifies to the canonical authority which it enjoyed.[8]

---

[4] Can. 77—Bruns, *Canones Apostolorum et Conciliorum Saeculorum IV–VII* (2 vols., Berlin, 1839), II, p. 12; hereafter referred to as Bruns.

[5] Cf. P. Hinschius, *Das Kirchenrecht der Katholiken und Protestanten in Deutschland* (6 vols., Berlin, 1869–1897), II, 263.

[6] "Plures baptismales ecclesiae in una terminatione esse non possunt sed una tantummodo cum capellis suis."—c. 54, C. XVI, q. 1. Burchard of Worms († 1025), *Decretorum Libri Viginti, lib.* III, c. 22—Migne, *Patrologiae Cursus Completus, Series Latina* (221 vols., Parisiis, 1844–1864), CXL, 677 (hereafter referred to as *MPL*). Ivo of Chartres (1040–1117), *Decretum,* Pars III, cap. 47—*MPL,* CLXI, 204. Friedberg (1837–1910) in his edition of the *Corpus Iuris Canonici* notes that the origin of this canon is uncertain, although Gratian ascribed it to a certain council of Toledo, while both Burchard and Ivo attributed it to a certan council of Aix-la-Chapelle.

[7] Jaffé, *Regesta Pontificum Romanorum ab condita Ecclesia ad annum MCXCVIII* (2. ed. [by Kaltenbrunner (to the year 590), Ewald (from 590 to 882), and Loewenfeld (from 882 to 1198), and so referred to as JK, JE and JL], 2 vols. in 1, Lipsiae, 1885–1888), JK, n. 139.

[8] Burchard, *Decretorum Libri Viginti,* Lib. III, c. 43—*MPL,* CXL, 680;

For the sake of a more orderly development, the functions of the "*presbyter parochianus*" will be studied individually, as they are treated in the *Corpus Iuris Canonici*, and an effort will be made to show whether and how they pertained exclusively to the pastor.

Article 2. *Baptism*

The conferral of solemn baptism was the cardinal function upon which rested the superiority of the *presbyter parochianus* over the priests of the lower churches. Throughout the fifth and sixth centuries, however, the pastor was limited by certain restrictions in his exercise of this function. In the first place, the bishop was still regarded, in the particular legislation of that period, as the ordinary minister of solemn baptism: only in the event that the bishop should be impeded, or should see fit to relinquish this right, could the pastor licitly administer solemn baptism.[9] Furthermore, baptism was to be conferred, except in the case of danger of death, only at the customary time of the Pasch or Pentecost.[10] The chrism used in the administration of the sacrament had to be that which was consecrated by the bishop of the diocese: it was the duty of the pastor to secure the chrism, either personally or through some other priest, before Easter.[11]

Ivo, *Decretum,* Pars III, cap. 47—*MPL,* CLXI, 208; *Panormia,* Lib. II, cap. 42—*MPL,* CXLI, 1091.

[9] *Capitula Collecta a Martino Episcopo Bracarensi,* cc. 52-53—Mansi, *Sacrorum Conciliorum Nova et Amplissima Collectio* (53 vols. in 60, Parisiis, 1901-1927), IX, 856-857 (hereafter referred to as Mansi); Hardouin, *Acta Conciliorum et Epistolae Decretales ac Constitutiones Summorum Pontificum* (12 vols., Parisiis, 1714-1715), III, 461 (hereafter referred to as Hardouin); Labbé-Cossart, *Sacrosancta Concilia ad regiam editionem exacta* (15 vols. in 16, Parisiis, 1671-1674), IX, 856. Cf. also the Council of Seville (619), c. 7—Mansi, X, 559; Hardouin, III, 560.

[10] Council of Autun (578), canon 18—Mansi, IX, 914; II Council of Mâcon (585), canon 3—*Monumenta Germaniae Historica* (*MGH*) (188 vols. incomplete, Hanoverae, 1826–), *Leges in 4;* Sectio III (*Concilia*), I (ed. F. Maassen, 1893), 166.

[11] *Statuta Ecclesiae Antiqua* (a conciliar collection which probably originated in Arles at the end of the fifth century, consisting of the more important enactments of Greek, African and Gallican councils arranged systematically, and of some fragments of Papal decretals), canon 36—Bruns, I, 145; Burchard, *Decretorum Libri Viginti,* lib. IV, c. 76—*MPL,*

In the fourth and fifth centuries the administration of baptism was shared by the bishop and the pastors of the baptismal churches. With the sixth century, however, the function of baptizing was almost completely relinquished by the bishop, and the parish priest of the rural baptismal churches gained recognition as the ordinary minister of this sacrament.[12]

In the development of the parochial right to baptize, as well as of parochial rights in general, the influence contributed by the medieval Germanic institution known as the " Proprietary Church " (EIGENKIRCHE) cannot be overlooked.[13] These were privately owned churches which sprang up on the estates of the Frankish kings and nobles during the Merovingian period. The proprietary churches were based on the Germanic concept that a private individual could own a church.[14] This was in sharp contradiction to the canonical tradition of antiquity, in which private ownership of ecclesiastical property was unknown.[15]

The proprietary churches in time acquired the parochial rights which had belonged to the old rural parishes on the countryside—the "*ecclesiae baptismales*"—through the use of the "*Bannus*." Just as the nobleman had succeeded in forcing the people living on his estate to have their corn ground in his mill, under penalty of a "*bannus*," or monetary fine, in like manner he secured for his

---

CXL, 741; Ivo, *Decretum*, Pars I, cap. 270—*MPL*, CLXI, 122; c. 123, D. IV, *de cons.*

[12] Cf. Pilatus, *Origines Iuris Pontificii ad Carolum Sextum* (Tridenti, 1739), lib. II, tit. 2; cf. also Waldron, *The Minister of Baptism*, The Catholic University of America Canon Law Studies, n. 170 (Washington, D. C.: The Catholic University of America Press, 1942), p. 31.

[13] Cf. U. Stutz, *Realenzyklopädie für protestantische Theologie und Kirche* (3. ed., 24 vols., Leipzig, 1890-1913), XXIII, 364-377. For a substantial English translation of the article, "Die Eigenkirche als Element des mittelalterlichgermanischen Kirchenrechtes, by the same author, cf. G. Barraclough, *Medieval Germany, 911-1250*, 2 vols. (Oxford: Blackwell and Mott, Ltd., 1938), II, 35-70.

[14] Cf. c. 3 of the *Capitula Ecclesiastica* which Charlemagne (742-814) supposedly issued at Salz: "Quicumque voluerit in sua proprietate ecclesiam aedificare, una cum consensu et voluntate episcopi in cujus parrochia fuerit licentiam habet"—*MGH*, Legum Section II (*Capitularia Regum Francorum*), I (ed. A. Boretius, Hanoverae, 1883), 119.

[15] Cf. P. Imbart de la Tour, *De Ecclesiis Rusticanis Aetate Carolingica* (Burgdigalae, 1890), Pars III, cap. 2, pp. 102-107.

church a monopoly over the spiritual needs of his serfs and vassals. His purpose in doing this was altogether mercenary: all the offerings, tithes and other donations belonged to him as owner of the church. The proprietary church was for the most part a highly lucrative investment. The financial implications of parochial rights were cast in strong relief by the proprietary church system.

During the tenth and eleventh centuries, the strictly parochial nature which the administration of baptism had acquired is clearly delineated in further legislation provoked by the encroachment of monasteries upon this function.[16] Evidence of the struggle which took place to vindicate the parochial right against monastic infringements is found in the *Decretum* of Gratian († ca. 1160). There is contained in this collection a decretal of Pope St. Gregory the Great (590–604) to Secundinus, bishop of Taormina, commanding that the baptismal font be removed from a certain monastery, "*propter molestias monachorum.*" [17] It is apparent that this phrase may be interpreted in one of two possible ways. According to one interpretation, the monks were the object of the annoyances or vexations, caused no doubt by the faithful seeking baptism at their font. The other interpretation would see in the monks the source of the annoyances, due to their indiscriminate and illicit administration of the sacrament. Joannes Teutonicus († 1245), who compiled the *Glossa ordinaria* of the *Decretum* around the year 1215, subscribed to the former interpretation.[18] A more critical text of the letter, however, carries the phrase, "*propter monachorum insolentias,*" which leaves no doubt as to the cause of the trouble.[19] Evidently the financial donations made by the faithful on the occasion of baptism constituted a very strong temptation for those who did not have the proper authorization. Another decretal of uncertain origin, found in Gratian and ascribed

[16] Cf. Council of Poitiers (1100), canon 10: "Ut nullus monachorum parochiale ministerium, id est, baptizare . . . praesumat"—Mansi, XX, 1124; Ivo, *Decretum*, Pars VII, cap. 150—*MPL*, CLXI, 581.

[17] C. 7, C. XVIII, q. 2; JE, n. 1261.

[18] "In monasterio Sancti Andreae erat baptisterium, cujus occasione monachi patiebantur molestias et incursionem populorum"—s.v. *pridem* in c. 7, C. XVIII, q. 2.

[19] *MGH, Epistolae* (7 vols., 1887–1928), Tomus 1, pars. 2 (ed. Ewald and Hartmann, Berlin, 1891), 215–216.

to Pope Eugene I (655–657), forbade monks to go abroad, for the sake of filthy lucre, to baptize.[20]

From the foregoing documents one may readily perceive how the administration of baptism had become deeply entrenched among the functions reserved to the parochial churches. The restriction which the law imposed on the activity of monks did not exclude the possibility that a monastery could acquire a proprietary church with parochial rights and thus could licitly possess a font and baptize. This could be accomplished by an "*incorporatio,*" that is, by means of a union of benefices through the subjection of one to the other.[21] The actual care of such parishes was in the hands of a vicar, very often a secular priest appointed by the bishop with the consent of the abbot.[22] Rufinus († ca. 1190), one of the earliest and more important commentators on the *Decretum* of Gratian (he wrote his commentary around the years 1157–1159), declared that certain monasteries had acquired parochial rights (*ius diocesianum*); he laid the blame for the adverse legislation to the audacity of certain monks who presumed to exercise parochial functions without the necessary authorization of the bishop.[23]

As late as the ninth century the city was not divided into parishes. This parochial unity of the city (*civitas*) was one of the most characteristic marks of the ancient diocese. The cathedral was the only parish church in the city. Around the ninth century, however, other parishes appeared in the city, administered by collegiate chapters.[24] Just as the cathedral chapter was pastor of the cathedral parish, so the other collegiate chapters exercised the

---

[20] C. 8, C. XVI, q. 1: ". . . ut nullus monachorum pro lucro terreno de monasterio exire . . . neque baptizare. . . ."

[21] U. Berlière, "L'Exercice du Ministère Paroissial par les Moines du XIIe au XVIIe Siècle," *Revue Bénédictine,* XXXIX (1927), 348–351.

[22] C. 1, X, *de capellis monachorum et aliorum religiosorum,* III, 37; Council of Nîmes (1096), canon 1—Mansi, XX, 933; cf. also canon 16 of the I General Council of the Lateran (1123)—*MGH,* Legum Sectio IV (*Constitutiones*), I (ed. L. Weiland, 1893), 576.

[23] *Die Summa Decretorum des Magister Rufinus,* editio H. Singer (Paderborn, 1902), ad C. XVI, q. 1, pp. 353–354.

[24] Thomassinus, *Vetus et Nova Ecclesiae Disciplina* (3 vols., Parisiis, 1688), Pars I, lib. II, capita 10, 11.

parochial ministry in a definite section of the city, and acquired parochial rights, including the rights of baptism, for that territory. In many instances, however, the cathedral chapter succeeded in preserving a cumulative competency along with the other parishes.[25]

Article 3. *Attendance at Mass*

The advent of the parochial system by no means put an end to the activity of the lower churches which hitherto had ministered to the faithful in the countryside. These, together with the chapels and oratories which had been erected by monastic communities or on the estates of the wealthy, continued to function, although dependently upon the baptismal churches. Mass continued to be celebrated in these lower churches and evidently the parishioners continued to assist at the Holy Sacrifice in these conveniently located chapels and oratories, to the detriment of the parish church. It was therefore to safeguard the very existence of the parochial church that abundant legislation was enacted, commanding the faithful to assist at Mass in the parish church on certain days of the year. As a typical example of such legislation, canon 21 of the Council of Agde (506) may be cited; it permitted the faithful to satisfy the obligation of assisting at Mass in rural oratories except on certain major feast days, on which days the people had to assist at Mass, either in the cathedral, or in one of the parochial churches.[26]

The requirements became more exacting in a later period, when it was forbidden to go to any but one's own parish church on these major feasts, and the number of feasts themselves was increased and the Sundays also were included. Evidence of these later restrictions is found in a number of *Paleae* inserted in the *Decretum.* Two are ascribed to a certain spurious council of Nantes, commonly believed to have been held at the end of the

[25] "Le Sacrament de Baptême," *Analecta Juris Pontificii* (Romae, 1855-1869; Parisiis, 1872-1891), VIII (1866), 1573-1604.

[26] Mansi, VIII, 328; Bruns, II, 150. Cf. also the I Council of Orleans (511), canon 25—Bruns, II, 165. For more detailed information concerning the functions of rural oratories after the advent of the baptismal churches, one may consult Feldhaus, *Oratories,* The Catholic University of America Canon Law Studies, n. 42 (Washington, D. C.: The Catholic University of America, 1927), pp. 36 sqq.

ninth century.[27] The laws ascribed to this council forbade priests to allow another's parishioner to assist at Mass in his church on Sundays and holydays. To this end the priest was instructed to ask the congregation, before beginning Mass, if there were any present who belonged to another parish. If so, they had to furnish some indication that they had received the permission of their proper pastor; otherwise they were to be ushered out and thus forced to return to their own parish church.[28]

Although their origin is uncertain, these *Paleae* are found incorporated in many canonical collections, solid evidence of the widespread legal force which they enjoyed in the early Middle Ages, when the concept of the parish was not yet clear-cut, and stringent regulations were needed to prevent confusion.[29] So effective were they that by the end of the twelfth century it was recognized as a well established parochial right that the faithful had to assist at Mass in their proper parish church, at least on certain feasts, the specification of which varied according to the different localities.[30]

The infringement, if any, by monasteries upon this parochial right had evidently been of a passive and negligible character, insufficient to warrant further laws. With the founding of the Mendicant Orders in the twelfth century, the violations of this right became more prevalent. For these new religious communities were of an active as well as a contemplative character, and it frequently happened that in their zeal for the care of souls they overstepped the limits of their constitutions and of the privileges accorded them. As a result there arose conflicts in which parish priests contended with the friars for the preservation of their ancient rights.

Pope Sixtus IV (1471–1484) found it necessary in 1478 to

---

[27] Cf. P. Fournier—G. LeBras, *Histoire des Collections Canoniques en Occident* (2 vols., Paris, Recueil Sirey, 1931), I, 259.

[28] C. 4, 5, C. IX, q. 2.

[29] Regino of Prüm († 915), *Libri Duo de Synodalibus Causis*, lib. II, cap. 61—*MPL*, CXXXII, 203; Burchard, *Decretorum Libri Viginti*, lib. II, cap. 91, 92—*MPL*, CXL, 642.

[30] "Habet autem hoc ius ecclesia in parochia sua, videlicet, ut populus pro divinis officiis illuc debeat convenire, et maxime in maioribus solemnitatibus"—Bernard of Pavia († 1213), *Summa Decretalium* (ed. E. A. T. Laspeyres, Ratisbonae, 1860), lib. III, tit. 25, p. 104.

intervene in one such dispute which was being waged between the Dominicans, Franciscans, and Carmelites on the one hand, and the prelates and rectors of churches in the town of Esslingen, of the diocese of Constance. In his decree the pontiff sharply rebuked the friars for proclaiming to the people that they were not bound to hear Mass in their parish churches on Sundays and holydays.[31]

In all fairness it must be stated that the Mendicant Orders were probably as much sinned against in this respect as they themselves offended. The supporters of parochial rights maintained for their part that if parishioners heard Mass in the churches of the Friars on Sundays and other days of obligation, they did not satisfy the precept. Their teaching caused so much anxiety among the faithful that Leo X (1513–1521) found it necessary in 1517 to allay all fears by giving assurance that the obligation of hearing Mass could be satisfied in the churches of the Mendicant Orders.[32]

With the spread of the mendicant orders and the consequent erection of more and more churches and oratories, the obligation of assisting at Mass in one's parish church gradually slackened in binding force and eventually became no more than a simple admonition. The first official indication that this change had taken place is had as early as the Council of Trent (1545–1563).[33]

Article 4. *Penance*

The history of penance in the Church of antiquity and of the early Middle Ages is one which for the most part still lies hidden in obscurity. The whole question of the ancient penitential procedure has provided many problems, upon which Catholic scholars

---

[31] "Quodque fratres Mendicantes non praedicent populos parochianos non teneri audire Missam in eorum parochiis diebus festivis et dominicis, quum iure sit cautum illis diebus parochianos teneri audire Missam in eorum parochiali ecclesia, nisi forsan ex honesta causa ab ipsa ecclesia se absentarent"—c. 2, *de treuga et pace,* I, 9, in Extravag. com.

[32] *Bullarum Diplomatum et Privilegiorum Sanctorum Romanorum Pontificum Taurinensis Editio* (24 vols., et Appendix, Augustae Taurinorum, 1857–1872), V, 710 (hereafter referred to as *Bull. Rom.*).

[33] Sess. XXII, *Decretum de observandis et evitandis in celebratione Missae.*

are still fundamentally divided.[34] Thomassinus (1619–1695) was of the opinion that priests were permitted to hear confessions from the earliest centuries; only the more serious and notorious sins had to be submitted to the bishop.[35] However, at some point of time in the early Middle Ages the power of hearing confessions became vested in parish priests to the exclusion of other priests, so that the Christian had to go to his proper pastor to receive absolution.[36]

The earliest evidence of this exclusive competency of the pastor in the administration of the sacrament of penance is found in a certain *Palea* inserted in the *Decretum* of Gratian.[37] Although it is ascribed to Pope Urban II (1088–1099), this *Palea* has been traced by Friedberg to the *Collectio Anselmo Dedicata,* composed towards the end of the ninth century, and from thence to the *Collectio Hibernensis* (ca. 800).[38]

In itself the wording of the text is not a strong argument for the reservation of penance to the parish priest; it is the interpreta-

---

[34] The question of private penance alone is one which still awaits a definite solution. It is the opinion of some scholars that private penance has always been in use from the earliest centuries, but there are others who maintain that private penance cannot be found before the fifth century. Cf. P. Palmer, "Jean Morin and the Problem of Private Penance," *Theological Studies,* VI (1945), 317–357; P. Galtier, *L'Eglise et la Remission des Pêches aux Premiers Siècles* (Paris, G. Beauchesne, 1932), pp. 217–226; B. Poschmann, *Die abendländische Kirchenbusse im Ausgang des christlichen Altertums* (München, J. Kösel & F. Pustet, 1928), p. 208.

[35] *Vetus et Nova Ecclesiae Disciplina,* Pars I, lib. II, cap. 23, n. 4.

[36] Cf. Burchard of Worms, *Decretorum Libi Viginti,* XIX, c. 2—*MPL,* CXL, 949; Regino of Prüm, *De Disciplinis Ecclesiasticis Libri Duo,* I, c. 309—*MPL,* CXXXII, 253.

[37] "Placuit, ut deinceps nulli sacerdotum liceat quemlibet commissum alteri sacerdoti ad penitentiam suscipere sine eius consensu, cui se prius commisit, nisi pro ignorantia illius, cui poenitens prius confessus est."—c. 3, D. VI, *de poenit.*

[38] "Anselmus in fine lib. VIII citat ex Hibernensi, et videtur error ex eo evenisse quod apud eundem Anselmum caput quoddam Urbani praetermittatur."—Friedberg, ad c. 2, C. IX, q. 2. For details concerning the *Collectio Anselmo Dedicata* and the *Collectio Hibernensis,* cf. Van Hove, *Commentarium Lovaniense in Codicem Iuris Canonici,* Vol. I, Tomus I, *Prolegomena* (2. ed., Mechliniae, Romae: H. Dessain, 1945), pp. 232, 290–291 (hereafter cited *Prolegomena*).

tion of the glossators which constitutes it as such. Concerning the phrase, for example, "*cui se prius commisit,*" which, as it stands, can lend itself to more than one meaning, the *Glossa ordinaria* has this to say: ". . . *i[s] cuius parochianus est. Ab alio enim non potest ligari vel solvi,*" and then refers the reader to c. 12, X, *de poenitentiis et remissionibus,* V, 38, which contains the famous decree, "*Omnis utriusque sexus,*" of the IV General Council of the Lateran (1215). Since this *Palea* gains all its force from a thirteenth century interpretation, it is impossible to argue that, since the text can be traced back to a ninth century collection, therefore the administration of the sacrament of penance was an exclusive parochial function as early as then.

Unmistakable evidence that the power to forgive sins was reserved to the proper pastor is had only with the IV General Council of the Lateran, held in 1215 under Pope Innocent III (1198–1216).[39] The general law enacted in Chapter 21 of the Lateran Council enjoined upon all adult Catholics the duty of approaching their pastor at least once a year, and of confessing their sins to him.[40]

Although the reason for the law is not given, a glance at the historical background in which the IV General Council of the Lateran convened may readily suggest one probable cause. In almost every diocese in the Holy Roman Empire conflicts waxed strong between the bishops and pastors, on the one hand, and the members of the newly established Mendicant Orders, who by virtue of their eloquent preaching and the broad powers which they claimed by apostolic privilege were attracting the faithful to

[39] That there must have been particular statutes to this effect before 1215 is indicated in the *Liber Poenitentialis* of Alanus de Insulis († 1202): "Si vero alterius sacerdotis parochianus ad alium accedat, ille ad quem accedit, si hoc sciat, ad proprium sacerdotem remittat; si vero cognoscat eum proprio sacerdoti confessum fuisse, ejus confessionem non respuat."—*MPL,* CCX, 299.

[40] "Omnis utriusque sexus fidelis, postquam ad annos discretionis pervenerit, omnia sua solus peccata confiteatur fideliter, saltem semel in anno, proprio sacerdoti, et iniunctum sibi poenitentiam studeat pro viribus adimplere, . . ."—Mansi, XX, 1007; c. 12, X, *de poenitentiis et remissionibus,* V, 38; Schroeder, *Disciplinary Decrees of the General Councils, Text, Translation and Commentary* (St. Louis: Herder, 1937), 258 and 570 (hereafter cited as Schroeder).

attendance at their own churches, to the detriment of the parish churches.[41]

The law of the IV Lateran Council corrected this harmful effect to a certain extent by granting to pastors the exclusive function of hearing the confessions of his parishioners at least once a year. Henceforth, no parishioner could seek absolution at least on this occasion from any priest other than his pastor, unless he had the permission of the latter to do so. This included the Mendicant Friars, as Bernard of Parma († 1266) noted in the *Glossa ordinaria.*[42] The privilege, wrote Bernard, which they had received from the Pope gave them the jurisdiction to exercise their priestly power, "*ordinis executionem sacerdotalis,*" but in no way made them equivalent to those who had been appointed by the bishop to be the pastors of the faithful.[43]

Lawrence the Spaniard wrote his commentary to Gratian's *Decretum* some time before the IV General Council of the Lateran (1215) and he naturally interpreted the *Palea* previously mentioned [44] in the light of the current law.[45] To the exception which is contained in the *Palea,* and which permits a parishioner to go to some other priest for absolution when his own pastor is not sufficiently learned to handle his case, Lawrence agreed, but he

[41] The first record of such an apostolic privilege being conceded to a Mendicant Order is that which Gregory IX granted to certain members of the Dominican Order, empowering them to absolve the sins of all lay people who confessed to them; Const. *Quoniam,* 10 maii, 1227—Potthast, *Regesta Pontificum Romanorum inde ab anno post Christum natum MCXCVIII ad annum MCCCIV* (2 vols., Berolini, 1874–1875), n. 7896 (hereafter cited Potthast). But, as the tenor of the Constitution indicates, serious disputes had already taken place between the religious and the secular clergy. For a conspectus of the privileges granted to religious, cf. Shuhler, *Privileges of Regulars to Absolve and Dispense,* The Catholic University of America Canon Law Studies, n. 186 (Washington, D. C.: The Catholic University of America Press, 1943), 1–24.

[42] C. 12, X, *de poenitentiis et remissionibus,* V, 38.

[43] ". . . privilegium non aequiparat eos illis, qui a populo sint electi, vel illis qui ab episcopo populo praeficiuntur, et dat eis solam executionem, et ita necessaria est adhuc licentia proprii sacerdotis, ut hic dicitur. . . . Nec Papa per talem indulgentiam intendit praeiudicare proprio sacerdoti."—c. 12, X, *de poenitentiis et remissionibus,* V, 38, s.v. *alieno sacerdoti.*

[44] C. 3, D. VI, *de poenit.*

[45] Cf. Van Hove, *Prolegomena,* p. 430 (n. 416).

doubted the utility of such a confession on practical grounds.[46] Lawrence was contradicted by Bernard of Parma, for Bernard insisted that the permission of the pastor had to be obtained even in the case in which his own ignorance rendered him incompetent to care for his parishioner.[47]

The decretal *Omnis utriusque sexus* had little effect in calming the disputes between the diocesan clergy and the friars. The friars continued to exercise their privilege of hearing the confessions of those who came to them, even during Lent. Some parishioners even ventured to make their Easter confession to a friar, without obtaining due permission from the proper pastor. This led many a pastor to suspect, with consequent ill-feeling, that the friars were enticing his parishioners away from him. On the other hand, the friars were subjected to bitter verbal onslaughts which attacked not only their privileges, but even their very reason for being friars.[48]

Boniface VIII (1294–1303) in his decretal, *Super cathedram,* of February 18, 1300, sought to subdue the storm by inculcating certain regulations to be observed by the mendicant orders with regard to the hearing of confessions. The religious superior was to present to the local ordinary for approbation certain friars whom he considered suitable for the hearing of confessions. If the latter rejected them, another suitable group was to be selected and presented. If these too were rejected, the rejection was automatically overruled, and the friars could lawfully hear confessions in that diocese in virtue of jurisdiction accredited directly by the Holy See.[49]

---

[46] C. 3, D. VI, *de poenit.*, s.v. *pro ignorantia.*

[47] C. 12, X, *de poenitentiis et remissionibus,* V, 38, s.v. *proprio sacerdoti.*

[48] Typical of such attacks was the pamphlet, "*De Periculis Novissimorum Temporum,*" written by William of St. Amour († 1272), canon theologian of the University of Paris. It was condemned by Alexander IV (1254–1261) in 1256—*Bull. Rom.,* III, 644 ff.

[49] Const. *Super Cathedram,* as found in c. 2, *de sepulturis,* III, 7, in Clem; Potthast, n. 24913. Benedict XI (1303–1304) went even further than his predecessor: he decreed that all priests religious who were deemed suitable by their superiors could lawfully hear the confessions of the faithful everywhere, without presentation to the local ordinary—Const. *Inter cunctas,* c. 1, *de privilegiis,* V, 7, in Extravag. com. This Constitution was abrogated by Clement V (1305–1314) in the Council of Vienne (1311–1312), and the

But the struggle did not cease. The peace of the Church continued to be disturbed sporadically by charges and countercharges between pastors and friars. There developed a school of thought which sought to strengthen the position of the pastors by maintaining that his permission was necessary for the validity of the sacrament when a parishioner confessed to another priest. In the early fourteenth century, a certain Master of Theology at the University of Paris named John of Pouilly (died after 1322) openly taught that such confessions were invalid, and that the sins thus confessed had to be re-submitted in confession to the pastor for absolution. His teaching was condemned by John XXII (1316–1334) in 1321 as erroneous, false and contrary to the Catholic Faith.[50] The condemnation was repeated by Eugene IV (1431–1447).[51]

That the regulars were not entirely blameless is evident from the severe rebuke which Sixtus IV administered to them in 1478: "Quod etiam ipsi Mendicantes desistant praedicare quod parochiani non sunt obligati, saltem in Paschate proprio confiteri sacerdoti, quia de iure tenetur parochianus saltem in Paschate proprio confiteri sacerdoti." [52] The disputes continued until the Council of Trent (1545–1563), when a definite solution was finally reached.

Article 5. *Holy Communion*

There is a scarcity of material in the canonical collections of antiquity concerning the parochial aspect of the administration of Holy Communion. Particular legislation of the period as recorded in Gratian's *Decretum* manifests the maternal solicitude which the Church ever bore towards the sick, rebuking the indifference of priests who sent Holy Communion to the sick through the agency of lay folk, even women.[53] Another particular law, also recorded

---

Constitution of Boniface VIII was re-affirmed—const. *Dudum*—C. 2, *de sepulturis*, III, 7, in Clem.

[50] Const. *Vas electionis*, as found in c. 2, *de haereticis*, V, 3, in *Extravag. com.*

[51] Const. *Gregis Nobis*, 16 ian. 1446—*Bull. Rom.*, V, 84 ff.

[52] C. 2, *de treuga et pace*, I, 9, in Extravag. com.

[53] C. 29, D. II, *de cons.*

in Gratian, warned priests to have the Holy Eucharist ever ready, so as to be prepared to minister to any parishioner when he became dangerously ill.[54] But there is no indication that the pastor enjoyed exclusive prerogatives in the administration of this sacrament.

As long as the faithful were permitted to assist at Mass in the lower churches and private or semi-public oratories, they were also permitted to receive Holy Communion there. In the seventh century the administration of Holy Communion became a strictly parochial function, at least on Sundays and on certain major feast days, when the faithful were obliged to attend Mass in their own parish church.[55] The legislation which forbade pastors to admit the parishioners of another to the celebration of the sacred mysteries served to strengthen the parochial nature of the administration of Holy Communion.[56]

In 1215, the IV General Council of the Lateran commanded all the faithful to receive the Holy Eucharist at least during Eastertime.[57] There had been previous legislation which prescribed the reception of Holy Communion on certain feasts, or a certain number of times each year, but without any explicit reference to the pastor.[58] Now for the first time the pastor was legally granted discretionary powers over the administration at least of the obligatory Easter Communion. Whether a parishioner should fulfill this precept, or should defer it temporarily, was left to the pastor to decide. The law was fortified with a severe penalty.[59]

In the *Glossa ordinaria* to this decretal, Ioannes Andreae († 1348) commented that the permission of the pastor was neces-

[54] C. 93, D. II, *de cons.*

[55] The campaign against private oratories continued well into the ninth century, as is evident from canon 47 of the Council of Paris (829)—*MGH*, Legum Section III (*Concilia*), Tomus II, Pars II (recensuit A. Werminghoff, Hannoverae et Lipsiae, 1908), 641.

[56] Thus Thomassinus explained one reason for these laws: "Ut ne videlicet quos proprius parochus sacris interdixerat, aut ad tempus abstinuerat, ii parocho ab alio fraudulenter et impune admitterentur ad synaxin et ad communionem."—*Vetus et nova Ecclesiae Disciplina*, Pars I, lib. II, cap. 24, n. 5.

[57] C. 12, X, *de poenitentiis et remissionibus*, V, 38.

[58] C. 16, 17, 19, D. II, *de cons.*

[59] ". . . alioquin et vivens ab ingressu ecclesiae arceatur, et moriens christiana careat sepultura."—c. 12, X, *de poenitentiis et remissionibus*, V, 38.

sary in order that any other priest might perform reserved functions, such as the administration of Holy Communion. He then posed the question whether or not this permission could be secured from the bishop rather than from the pastor, and answered in the affirmative, though somewhat hesitantly. He argued that the diocese was the parish of the bishop, and therefore the bishop could most certainly grant this permission when a parish in the diocese was vacant. The permission could also be sought from the bishop when the parish was occupied by a pastoral incumbent, but the commentator sagely counselled against such a practice.[60]

The provisions of the law enacted in the canon "*Omnis utriusque sexus*" concerning Holy Communion were strongly emphasized in subsequent provincial councils, and thereby greater assurance was gained for a universal compliance with them.[61] In the Supplement to the *Summa Theologica* of Saint Thomas Aquinas (1225–1274) there is an indication of how thoroughly parochial the administration of Holy Communion had become, for the author found it necessary to affirm the validity of the sacrament also for the case in which is was administered by someone other than the pastor.[62]

Even after the promulgation of the canon *Omnis utriusque sexus* many questions still remained unanswered. Were the friars forbidden to distribute Holy Communion in their own churches to the faithful who requested it during the Paschal season? What precisely was the Paschal season?[63] Could Tertiaries and mem-

[60] *Glossa ordinaria,* in c. 1, *de privilegiis et excessibus privilegiatorum,* V 7, in Clem., s.v. *presbyteri.*

[61] Council of Cologne (1310), can. 20: "Statuimus item, ut nullus parochianus ab alio quam a suo vero plebano communionem recipiat, nisi de hoc privilegiis authenticis sit munitus"—Mansi, XXV, 242; Council of Avignon (1337), can. 4—Mansi, XXV, 1089; Council of Padua (1339), can. 12—Mansi, XXV, 1137.

[62] ". . . non licet eucharistiam ab alio quam a proprio sacerdote accipere, quamvis verum sit sacramentum quod ab alio percipitur"—*Supplementum,* q. 8, a. 4, ad 2.

[63] It was not until 1440 that Eugene IV (1431–1447) designated the period between Palm Sunday and Low Sunday inclusively for the fulfillment of the Paschal precept by the Church Universal—Ep. "*Fide digna,*" 8 iul. 1440—*Codicis Iuris Canonici Fontes,* cura Emi Petri Card. Gasparri editi (9 vols., Romae: Typis Polyglottis Vaticanis, 1923–1939; [vols. VII, VIII, IX, ed. cura et studio Emi Iustiniani Card. Serédi]), n. 53 (hereafter cited as *Fontes*).

bers of lay religious societies living a community life satisfy the precept through the ministry of their respective chaplains without the permission of their proper pastor?

The Council of Vienne (1311–1312) further buttressed parochial prerogatives by threatening the penalty of a "*latae sententiae*" excommunication against any religious who presumptuously administered the Holy Eucharist (*qui sacramentum Eucharistiae ministrare praesumpserint*) without permission of the proper pastor.[64] But just what is the meaning of the phrase "*sacramentum Eucharistiae ministrare?*" Certainly it included the administration of Holy Viaticum, for that function had always been undisputedly reserved to the parish priest, as will be pointed out in the following article. In the *Glossa ordinaria* the phrase was interpreted as meaning the administration of Holy Communion on Easter Sunday, "*in die Paschae.*"[65] But let it be supposed that a parishioner had already satisfied the Paschal precept, having received Holy Communion, for example, in his parish church on Palm Sunday. Could a priest religious give Holy Communion to such a one on Easter Sunday, without incurring the penalty of excommunication?

These and other difficulties were settled in successive decrees of the Holy See, all of them uncompromisingly upholding the right of the pastor in the consideration of the Paschal Communion, while otherwise conceding ample liberty to the friars in the administration of Holy Communion.[66] Only on Easter Sunday itself were the priests religious forbidden to administer Holy Communion to the faithful who requested it.[67] Privileges granted to Third Orders and lay religious in relation to the reception of Holy Communion invariably made explicit exception for the Paschal Communion.[68] There were instances, however, of privileges being granted to the nobility and to large hospitals, which privileges allowed the beneficiaries to fulfill the Paschal precept

---

[64] C. 1, *de privilegiis et excessibus privilegiatorum,* V, 7, in Clem.

[65] Casus ad c. 1, *de privilegiis et excessibus privilegiatorum,* V, 7, in Clem.

[66] Cf. *Bull. Rom.,* IV, 639; V, 689; V, 392.

[67] *Ibid.,* VI, 192, 399; IX, 249.

[68] *Ibid.,* IV, 639; V, 392, 689.

without having recourse to their proper pastor.[69] With these comparatively few exceptions, the reserved parochial character of the Paschal Communion remained unchanged through the centuries.

Article 6. *Holy Viaticum and Extreme Unction*

It seems probable that from antiquity the administration of Extreme Unction was attended to by priests, in accordance with the words of St. James, "Inducat presbyteros ecclesiae qui orent super eum ungentes eum oleo . . ."[70] With the development of parishes the spiritual care of those living in a definite territory became vested in the "*presbyter parochianus.*" He, assisted by a staff of clerics, administered to their needs.

Concerning the administration of the last Sacraments very little is recorded in the medieval canonical collections. There is sufficent evidence to warrant the assertion that the care of the sick and dying pertained exclusively to the pastor. In describing the pastoral functions of priests charged with the care of souls, the Council of Aix-la-Chapelle (836) emphasized the priests' duty of sedulously guarding the faithful confided to their care, and of seeing to it that they did not die without the last Sacraments.[71]

Disputes between pastors and religious arose concerning the administration of Extreme Unction as well as about other parochial activities. Pope Clement V (1305–1314) vindicated the right of pastors to administer Extreme Unction when he forbade religious under pain of excommunication to anoint anyone without first obtaining the permission of the proper pastor.[72] This measure, drastic though it may have been, still did not succeed in its purpose, and in 1516 Leo X found it necessary to reaffirm emphatically the

---

[69] *Ibid.*, IV, 110; E. Langlois, *Les Registres de Nicolas IV, Bibliotheque des Écoles francaises d'Athènes et de Rome*, 2 ser., t. 5. (Paris, 1886), n. 374; G. Mollat, Jean XXII, *Lettres Communes, Bibliotheque des Écoles francaises d'Athènes et de Rome*, 14 vols. in 11 (Paris, E. DeBoccard, 1904–1935), II, n. 7277; IV, n. 15792; VIII, n. 42863. Cf. also P. Browe, "Die Kommunion in der Pfarrkirche," *Zeitschrift für katholische Theologie*, LIII (1929), 486–489.

[70] James, V:14–15.

[71] *De Vita et Doctrina inferiorum ordinum*, canon 5—*MGH, Leges in 4*, Sectio III (*Concilia*), Tomus II, pars II, 711–712.

[72] C. 1, *de privilegiis et excessibus privilegiatorum*, V, 7, in Clem.

right of pastors in the administration of the last sacraments.[73] In 1648, Innocent X (1644–1655) upheld the parochial right;[74] and two hundred years later, in the Constitution "*Apostolicae Sedis*" of Pius IX, an excommunication reserved to the Holy See was directed against religious who presumed to administer the last Sacraments without due permission.[75]

Ordinarily Holy Viaticum and Extreme Unction were administered concomitantly to parishioners in danger of death. During the time of a general interdict pastors were forbidden, by command of Gregory IX, to administer Extreme Unction, although the administration of Holy Viaticum was permitted.[76] In order that Holy Viaticum might not be wanting to the dying, it was allowed to celebrate Mass once a week for the duration of the interdict.[77]

Article 7. *Matrimony*

Section 1. ASSISTANCE AT MARRIAGES

The functions which became exclusively reserved to pastors have their source in custom as well as in statutory law. Due to the complete absence of any early legislation concerning the pastor's exclusive right to assist at marriages, it seems probable that its origin is to be found in custom. It is true that during the fifth and sixth centuries, when the parochial system was gradually evolving, the blessing of the priest was required.[78] In the "*Capitularium Caroli Magni et Ludovici Pii,*" a collection dating back to the ninth century, there is an exposition of the procedure to be followed in marriages; here again the blessing of the priest is the prominent feature, and something is stated concerning the pastor's exclusive right to perform this function.[79]

---

[73] Const. "*Dum intra,*" 19 dec. 1516—*Fontes,* n. 72.

[74] Const. "*Cum Sicut*" 14 maii, 1648—*Fontes,* n. 232.

[75] *Collectanea S. Congregationis de Propaganda Fide* (2 vols., Romae, 1907), II, n. 1348.

[76] C. 11, X, *de poenitentiis et remissionibus,* V, 38.

[77] C. 57, X, *de sententia excommunicationis,* V, 39.

[78] *Statuta Ecclesiae Antiqua,* c. 13—Bruns, I, 143; c. 5, C. XXX, q. 5; c. 33, D. XXIII.

[79] VII, c. 179: "Sed prius conveniendus est Sacerdos in cujus parochia nuptiae fieri debent, in Ecclesia coram populo. Et ibi inquirere una cum

In the writings of the Decretalists, the assisting at marriages was without any hesitation listed as one of the parochial rights. Among the several powers which custom as well as legal enactment had reserved to the pastor, Bernard of Pavia (ca. 1198) mentioned the blessing of spouses, "*benedictiones sponsarum*"; he made no effort to distinguish from which of these two juridical sources each individual parochial right emanated.[80] Hostiensis († 1271) also listed the blessing of those who entered the married state as a parochial right.[81]

The infringements of religious orders provoked the first legal statute which unequivocally labelled assistance at marriages as a reserved parochial function. Evidently many friars had been assisting at marriages without regard for the right which custom had acknowledged to pastors. In the Council of Vienne (1311–1313) Clement V forbade religious, under pain of excommunication, to assist at marriages (*matrimonia solemnizare*) if they had not obtained the special permission of the pastor.[82]

Section 2. PUBLICATION OF THE BANNS

It is certain that the practice of publicly announcing future marriages in the church for the purpose of bringing to light any hidden obstacles to the union originated in the Gallican Church, around the end of the twelfth century. Many authors point to Archbishop Odo of Paris (1196–1208) as the first to prescribe the publishing of banns.[83] By the early part of the twelfth century

---

populo ipse Sacerdos debet si ejus propinqua sit, an non, an alterius uxor, vel sponsa, vel adultera. . . . Sed postquam ista omnia probata fuerint, et nihil impedierit, tunc si virgo fuerit, cum benedictione Sacerdotis, sicut in Sacramentario continetur. . . ."—Mansi, XVIIB, 1062; *MGH,* Leges, Tomus II[2] (ed. G. H. Pertz, Hannoverae, 1837—Unveränderter Neudruck, Leipzig: Verlag K. Hiersemann, 1925), p. 113.

[80] *Summa Decretalium,* III, 25 (commenting on X, *de parochiis et alienis parochianis,* III, 29).

[81] *Commentaria in V Libros Decretalium,* 3 vols. (Venetiis, 1581), Lib. III, tit. 29, *de parochiis et alienis parochianis,* c. un., n. 1.

[82] C. 1, *de privilegiis et excessibus privilegiatorum,* V, 7, in Clem.

[83] *Synodicae Constitutiones,* cap. VII, 1—Mansi, XXII, 679. Cf. Roberts, *The Banns of Marriage,* The Catholic University of American Canon Law Studies, n. 64 (Washington, D. C.: The Catholic University of America, 1931), p. 11.

the practice was widespread throughout the Frankish Empire, as is manifest from a letter of Pope Innocent III (1198–1216), dated October 29, 1212, referring to the banns as an institution proper to that region.[84]

A short time later, in the IV General Council of the Lateran, Pope Innocent III extended this particular law to the Universal Church in an effort to stamp out clandestine marriages.[85] There was no explicit statement that the function of publishing the banns was essentially parochial, though that would seem to be a valid inference, since to have any effect, the banns had to be published in the churches where the parties were known, that is, in their parish churches. Panormitanus (1386–1453) asserted that if the parties had lived in several parishes, the publications had to be made in each of the several parochial churches.[86] The *Glossa ordinaria* spoke of the duty of the "*parochialis sacerdos*" in seeing that the publication of the banns was carried out.[87]

From the fourteenth century to the Council of Trent there was no further development in the parochial rights with reference to the sacrament of matrimony.

Article 8. *Ecclesiastical Burial*

One finds the question of ecclesiastical burial abundantly treated in the *Corpus Iuris Canonici.*[88] Among the canons and decrees there contained, one, belonging to Pope Leo III (795–816), indicates that as early as the eighth century the parochial church had a definite, well established interest in the ecclesiastical burial of its parishioners.[89] The Pontiff prescribed that each one be buried in

---

[84] C. 27, X, *de sponsalibus et matrimoniis,* IV, 1; Potthast, n. 4614.

[85] Can. 51: "Quare specialem quorundam locorum consuetudinem ad alia generaliter prorogando, statuimus, ut, quum matrimonia fuerint contrahenda, in ecclesiis per presbyteros publice proponantur, competenti termino praefinito, ut infra illum, qui voluerit et valuerit, legitimum impedimentum opponat." c. 3, X, *de clandestina desponsatione,* IV, 3; Schroeder, pp. 280 and 578.

[86] *Commentaria in Quinque Libros Decretalium* (5 vols. in 7, Venetiis, 1588), Lib. IV, tit. 3, *de clandestina desponsatione,* c. 3, n. 7.

[87] *Glossa ordinaria,* in c. 3, X, *de clandestina desponsatione,* IV, 3, *casus.*

[88] C. XIII, q. 1, 2; X, *de sepulturis,* III, 28; *de sepulturis,* III, 12, in VI°; *de sepulturis,* III, 7, in Clem.

[89] C. 1, X, *de sepulturis,* III, 28—JE, n. 2536.

the burial place of his ancestors, after the manner of the ancient patriarchs; however, if one should express the wish to be buried elsewhere, this wish was to be respected, but in such a case a third part of all that was left in his last will to the church designated for his burial was to be given to that church "*in qua coelesti pabulo a principio sui exordii quotidie refici consuevit.*" [90]

From the text of this decretal it is seen that the parochial priest had a preferred claim to the right of conducting the burial. Bernard of Parma († 1266) interpreted this decretal in the sense that the ancestral tombs were within the limits of the parochial church, for he declared that the third part is due "illi ecclesiae . . . in qua sepeliri debeat, vel debebat sepeliri si non elegisset alibi sepultura(m), *et* ubi dum vivebat caelesti pabulo refici consuevit." [91] However, it seems more probable that the text should rather be understood in the sense that the church to which the ancestral tombs belonged had the right of burial, even if that should not have been the parish church. This view is substantiated by a decretal of Boniface VIII (1294–1303), which prescribed that, if one rejected the church of his ancestral tomb for another burial place, the canonical portion was nonetheless to be paid to the parish church, not to the church rejected.[92]

Another decretal of Boniface VIII gives some indication that a quasi-domicile did not afford sufficient title to permit a church to claim the right of conducting the burial. Considering the case of a man who died in his country home, outside the limits of his proper parish, the Pope declared that such a one was to be buried, not in the country church, "sed in sua parochiàli, vel in ea potius, in qua maiorum ipsius ab antiquo sepultura exstitit." [93]

The financial benefits accruing from this right were of no small importance. One may naturally suspect, therefore, that the pastors would not be left unmolested in their enjoyment of this right. And indeed there is extant a letter of Leo IX (1049–1054) in

---

[90] *Loc. cit.*

[91] *Casus* ad c. 1, X, *de sepulturis,* III, 28; the italics are those of the writer.

[92] C. 2, *de sepulturis,* III, 12, in VI°.

[93] *Ibid.,* c. 3. The *Glossa* simply comments: ". . . est portandus ad suam ecclesiam parochialem."—*casus* ad c. 3.

which he excoriated certain wicked abbots and monks who rapaciously seduced the laity so that, either while living or in their will, they might bequeath their goods to the monasteries, and thus leave nothing to their parish churches.[94] Alexander III (1159–1181) restricted the scope of this decretal by declaring that nothing needed to be given to the parish church when a parishioner entered a monastery or a religious order and thereupon turned over all his possessions to the community. However, if one entered while laboring under a sickness to which he eventually succumbed, the canonical portion had to be given to the parish church.[95] According to the glossators, the amount of the canonical portion was to be determined by local custom.

Gratian recorded an interesting case in his *Decretum*. He used it as a means to illustrate all the delicate complexities which his contemporaries were likely to encounter in determining various specific points in connection with the right of granting burial. The parishioners of a certain baptismal church (A) had moved into another parish (B) but they continued to cultivate their ancestral farms which were situated in the former parish (A). After fifty years had elapsed, the clerics of parish A brought suit against parish B, claiming that they still possessed the right to receive tithes and to give ecclesiastical burial to those who formerly had lived in their parish. They based their claim to give burial on excerpts from the writings of St. Jerome († 420) and St. Augustine († 430), which indicated that one ought to be buried in the tomb of his ancestors.[96] The defendants defeated this claim, however, by pointing to the law enacted in the Council of Tribur (895): ". . . ubi quis decimas persolvebat vivus, ibi sepeliatur mortuus."[97] This case reveals the intimate connection which existed in the twelfth century between the payment of personal tithes and the right to give ecclesiastical burial. The question of domicile was secondary.

The legislation contained in the Decretals of Gregory IX made

---

94 C. 2, X, *de sepulturis*, III, 28.

95 *Ibid.*, c. 4; JL, n. 9035.

96 C. 2, 3, C. XIII, q. 2.

97 C. 6, C. XIII, q. 2. Cf. Hefele-Leclercq, *Histoire des Conciles* (10 vols. in 19, Paris: Letouzey et Ané, 1907–1938), Vol. IV, Part II, p. 700.

no changes concerning the parochial right to conduct the ecclesiastical burial. In the *Glossa ordinaria* to the Decretals, Bernard of Parma noted that certain contemporary canonists maintained that, if one wished to reject his parish church as the place of burial, he had to choose a church that was "*magis religiosa,*" i.e., where prayers and masses were more frequently offered, as, for example, a monastery church. However, there were others, like Vincent and Lawrence, both of whom were Spanish canonists of the early thirteenth century, who held that one was free to choose any place of burial, even a church "*minus religiosa,*" provided that the canonical portion was duly rendered to the parochial church. Bernard favored the first opinion, though he conceded that any church that was "*minus religiosa*" could be allowed the right of burial by means of apostolic privilege, and cited the churches of the Knights Hospitallers, of the Knights Templars, and of the Dominicans, as examples.[98]

According to Panormitanus, if a pastor was negligent in seeking his canonical portion, the bishop himself could request it in the name of the parish church. Panormitanus based the bishop's right to intervene on the fact that in the ancient Church the bishop alone rightfully received and dispensed whatever was given to the church. Even though this administration had long since been relinquished to the parish priest, the native right still belonged to the bishop and could be exercised when the pastor showed negligence.[99]

In the year 1300, Boniface VIII granted to the churches of the Dominicans and Franciscans the right of "free" burial (*libera sepultura*), that is, the right to bury all who had chosen to receive burial in their churches.[100] This was the first of a series of

---

[98] *Glossa* in c. 3, X, *de sepulturis,* III, 28, s.v. *nova et minus religiosa.* An *additio,* probably from the pen of Iannes Andreae († 1348), commented: "Secunda opinio est hodie approbata."

[99] *Commentaria in Quinque Libros Decretalium,* Lib. III, tit. 28, *de sepulturis,* c. 3(2), n. 2.

[100] C. 2, *de sepulturis,* III, 7, in Clem; Potthast, n. 24913. To the *Glossa ordinaria* there is annexed an addition, probably of Francis de Zabarella (1335–1417), which defined "*liberam*" as signifying "quandam praerogativam absolutam et dominium super actu(m) cui adiicitur"—*additio,* ad

apostolic privileges which accorded to many religious orders the right of granting burial.[101] All these grants recognized the right of the parochial church to the canonical portion. The privilege which exempted them from this obligation was obtained by some religious orders. Thus a severe blow was dealt to the parochial right.[102]

---

c. 2. In other words, the privilege carried with it all the other powers intermediate to its use.

[101] C. un., *de iudiciis,* II, 1, in Extravag. com.; *Bull. Rom.,* III, 426; 741; IV, 572; V, 219; 421.

[102] *Bull. Rom.,* V, 349–350.

CHAPTER II

PAROCHIAL RIGHTS AND FUNCTIONS SINCE THE COUNCIL OF TRENT (1545–1563)

Article 1. *The Legislation of the Council of Trent* (1545–1563)

The Council of Trent (1545–1563) was convened by Pope Paul III (1534–1549) to effect a much needed reform throughout the Church. Being the basic unit in the ecclesiastical structure upon which the welfare of the whole organization depends, the parish and its problems came in for weighty discussion at the Council. The Fathers realized that parochial organization was essential for the spiritual well-being of the faithful. In order to eliminate the existing confusion, the Council commanded all bishops to assign clearly marked boundaries for the parishes, in such a manner that each parish be composed of the people in a certain definite territory, to whom one pastor was appointed to care for their spiritual needs. The pastor was to enjoy exclusive jurisdiction over the people assigned to him, and from him alone could they licitly receive the sacraments.[1]

Foremost among the parochial problems confronting the Council was the need for some harmonization between the apostolic privileges of regulars and the rights of pastors. Successive pontifical concessions to the mendicant orders, individually or collectively, had developed by intercommunication into the vast treasury of privileges known as the "*Mare Magnum.*" The resultant confusion in the ministry could be solved only by means of an authoritative clarification of rights and a precise definition of competency. This was the task which the Council appointed to itself and successfully accomplished.

[1] ". . . unicuique suum perpetuum peculiaremque parochum assignet, qui eas cognoscere valeat, et a quo solo licite sacramenta suscipiant. . . ." Sess. XXIV, *de ref.*, c. 13.

The clarification of the privileges of regulars made by the Council was wholly in the pastors' favor. Thus, for example, the privilege which many churches of regulars had acquired in the forty years before the Council of Trent, namely of keeping the funeral quarter share ("*quarta funeralium*") was abrogated in favor of the cathedral or parish church which had previously possessed the right to this canonical portion.[2] The Council also curtailed the broad powers to absolve, which had been granted to the friars, by prescribing that no one, not even a regular, could hear the confessions of layfolk without the approbation of the local ordinary, unless he held a parochial benefice.[3] This approval was necessary for the validity of the absolution which the confession called for. This requirement greatly enhanced the pastor's right over his parishioners with regard to the sacrament of penance.

In the decree *Tametsi*, the Council definitely placed the sacrament of matrimony and all that pertained to it within the class of reserved parochial functions. All the prerogatives which custom and particular law had conceded to the pastor in connection with safeguarding the proper administration of the sacrament of matrimony were here ratified and incorporated in the universal law of the Church.[4]

Concerning the banns, the Council simply reiterated the law enacted in the IV General Council of the Lateran (1215),[5] but with two notable differences. In the Tridentine decree it was explicitly stated that the banns were to be announced by the proper pastor of the contracting parties. Moreover, this publication was to take place on three successive days of obligation.[6]

---

[2] Sess. XXV, *de ref.*, c. 13.

[3] Sess. XXIII, *de ref.*, c. 15.

[4] Sess. XXIV, *de ref.*, c. 1.

[5] Can. 51; c. 3, X, *de clandestina desponsatione*, IV, 3.

[6] ". . . ter a proprio contrahentium parocho tribus continuis diebus festivis in ecclesia inter Missarum solemnia publice denuncietur. . . ."—Sess. XXIV, *de ref.*, c. 1. That it was the practice to announce the banns on three Sundays or holydays seems evident from a book of instructions written for parish priests about 1426, which is quoted by Abbot Gasquet, *Parish Life in Medieval England* (New York: Benziger Brothers, 1906), p. 209: "The seventh Sacrament is wedlock before the which Sacrament the banes in holy church shal be thrys asked on thre solempne days—a werk day or two between, at the lest. . . ."

The decree then proceeded to vindicate the pastor's exclusive right to assist at marriages, in a momentous declaration which revolutionized the very essence of the form in which the contracting of matrimony was to be executed. Thenceforth, declared the Council, matrimony could not be contracted validly except in the presence of the pastor, or of some other priest with the pastor's permission, and of two or three witnesses.[7] The same decree also explicitly confided the nuptial blessing to the exclusive competence of the pastor. He alone was authorized to impart the nuptial blessing, notwithstanding any custom, even though it be immemorial, to the contrary. No other priest could licitly assume this function without the permission either of the pastor or of the ordinary. If any priest dared, without the due permission of the proper pastor, either to assist at the marriage of those who were not his parishioners or to bestow on them the nuptial blessing, he automatically incurred a suspension in which he remained until he had been absolved by the ordinary of the proper pastor whose right he had violated.[8]

The effects of this decree were very far-reaching. Theretofore the authority of the pastor in the matter of safeguarding the fit and proper administration of the sacrament of matrimony had been somewhat vague, more or less according to the measure that custom and particular legislation wished to grant him, and never so far-reaching as to affect the validity of the sacrament's administration. Never before, in fact, had any function been reserved to the pastor in such manner as to prejudice its validity if the execution of the function was undertaken by someone else. Now, for the first time, he was given exclusive competence over the administration of a sacrament in such wise that his intervention was required under pain of nullity. The decree *Tametsi* constituted indeed a historic landmark in the development of reserved parochial functions.

A new function, somewhat similar to the publishing of the banns, was assigned in a general manner to pastors by the Council of Trent, and eventually became reserved to them exclusively. In setting forth the discipline to be observed in the administration of the sacrament of Holy Orders, the Council instructed bishops to

---

[7] Sess. XXIV, *de ref.*, c. 1.

[8] *Loc. cit.*

see to it that the names of candidates for major Orders be announced publicly in church. This was to be done either by the pastor or by some other person according as the bishop deemed it more suitable.[9] Under ordinary circumstances no one could be more suitable for discharging this function than the proper pastor of the candidate, as experience demonstrated.

No change was effected in the status of the other parochial rights. The provisions of the IV General Council of the Lateran concerning annual confession and communion were re-affirmed.[10] It was taken for granted that baptism was to be administered by the pastor of the one to be baptized.[11] Bishops were instructed to admonish the faithful to assist frequently at the divine mysteries in their parish church, at least on Sundays and on the more solemn feast days.[12] The old obligation to assist at Mass in one's own parish church had been softened in the course of time to a mere counsel.

On the whole the Council lent a very significant impetus to a more closely regulated discipline in the establishment of parochial life and in the fixation of parochial rights. The rights of pastors which had developed in the course of centuries were given the full approval of an authoritative confirmation, and were further extended, as in the matters that concerned the administration of the sacrament of matrimony. This procedure was wholly in conformity with the Council's purpose to encourage the growth of an orderly parochial system and a virile parochial life and activity.

Article 2. *Parochial Rights Since the Council of Trent*

With one exception, the parochial rights which in their fixation had become crystallized by the time of the Council of Trent underwent little or no change in the succeeding centuries. The one exception was the right which corresponded to the obligation of parishioners to assist at Mass in their parish church on Sundays and the principal feast days. There is an indication as early as

---

[9] Sess. XXIII, *de ref.*, c. 5.

[10] Sess. XXIII, *de ref.*, c. 9; sess. XIV, *de ref.*, c. 8.

[11] Sess. XIV, *de ref.*, c. 2.

[12] Sess. XXII, *Decretum de observandis et evitandis in celebratione Missae.*

the Council of Trent that this obligation had been relaxed.[13] The admonition enjoined by the Council partook more of the nature of a paternal counsel than of a legal sanction.[14]

The fact that this obligation had ceased to bind is noted by almost all the post-Tridentine authors.[15] Van Espen (1646–1728) was typical of a very small minority who maintained that the faithful were still legally bound to assist at Mass in their proper parish church.[16] This opinion quickly died out, so that Bouix (1808–1870), writing in the following century, did not even mention it in his list of parochial rights.[17]

The development which took place regarding the right to confer baptism concerned itself with specific practical points rather than with the right itself. The right was universally acknowledged; the application of the right in varying circumstances needed further clarification. One important question which had to be solved concerned the right of a cathedral church in relation to the right of the other parochial churches of the diocese.[18]

Many a pastor's right to baptize his own subjects was consid-

---

[13] *Loc. cit.*

[14] An example of the manner in which this admonition was executed may be seen in the decree of the VI Provincial Council of Milan (1582), held under St. Charles Borromeo (1538–1584), which read in part: ". . . con questo nostro avviso essortiamo, preghiamo e sconguriamo per le viscere di Nostro Signor Giesu Christo tutte e qual si voglia fedele, . . . che voglino (non ostante che habbino nelle vicinanze nelle ville e borghi, oratori cappelle, et altre chiese dove possono essere presenti al santissimo sacrificio della Missa) ciascuno nulladimeno sovente volte; almeno le Domeniche, et altre feste solemni venire alla sua chiesa parochiale. . . ."—*Acta Ecclesiae Mediolanensis,* cura et studio A. Ratti (3 vols. in 2, Mediolani, 1890–1892), II, Actorum Pars III, 1172.

[15] Barbosa, *De Officio et Potestate Parochi Descriptio,* ed. U. Giraldi a S. Cajetano (Romae, 1774), Pars I, cap. 11, n. 18; Pirhing, *Ius Canonicum Nova Methodo Explicatum* (5 vols., Dilingae, 1674–1678), Lib. I, tit. 31, n. 142; Schmalzgrueber, *Ius Ecclesiasticum Universum* (5 vols. in 12, Romae, 1843–1845), III, tit. 29, n. 11.

[16] *Ius Ecclesiasticum Universum* (10 vols., Venetiis, 1769), Pars II, sect. 1, tit. 5.

[17] *Tractatus De Parocho* (3. ed., Parisiis, 1880), Pars IV, cap. 1, n. 1, p. 437.

[18] Cf. "Le Sacrament de Baptême," *Analecta Iuris Pontificii,* VIII (1866), 1573–1604.

erably restricted by the cumulative or exclusive right which another pastor claimed to possess over the former's parishioners. This practice was of long duration, dating back to the period before the Council of Trent, when parochial organization was in its infancy. With the development of parishes, a new parish retained a filial relation to the mother church, and the pastor of the latter was acknowledged as possessing an equal right to confer baptism on the members of the filial church. In fact, many cathedrals had retained an exclusive right to baptize all the people of the town. In a number of decrees covering a period of two centuries, the Sacred Congregation of the Council gradually wiped out the claims of many cathedral churches to an exclusive baptismal right.[19]

While theoretically vindicating the parochial prerogatives with respect to the administration of the sacrament of penance, the Council of Trent indirectly paved the way for the weakening and ultimate dissolution of that parochial right. The Council declared that the pastor possessed ordinary jurisdiction over his parishioners in virtue of his appointment to the parochial benefice.[20] The Council also restrained the powers of regulars to absolve by demanding that they obtain, *ad validitatem,* the express approval of the bishop. But nonetheless parishioners could freely confess to regulars approved by the bishop, or to other pastors, without any special permission on the part of the proper pastor as a condition for the exercise of this option.[21]

In practice the rightful use of this liberty was extended during the succeeding generations even to the Easter Confession, which, according to the prescription of the decree *Omnis utriusque sexus,* had to be duly made to the "*sacerdos proprius.*"[22] Canonists justified this apparent violation of the law, explaining that the

[19] S. C. C., *Neapolitana,* 6 et 27 sept. 1687—*Fontes,* n. 2903; 21 febr., 28 aug. 1688—*Analecta Iuris Pontificii,* VIII (1866), 1590–1593; *Fabrianen.,* 24 maii, 21 iun. 1732—*Fontes,* n. 3392; 2 maii 1733—*Fontes,* n. 3401; 14 nov. 1733—*Fontes,* n. 3410; *Aesina,* 15 iul. 1797—*Fontes,* n. 3905. The series of responses to Fabriano offers a good illustration of the changing attitude of the Holy See towards exclusive baptismal rights.

[20] Sess. XXIII, *de ref.,* c. 15.

[21] Cf. addition of Giraldi of St. Cajetan to Barbosa, *De Officio et Potestate Parochi Descriptio,* Pars II, cap. 19, n. 3.

[22] C. 12, X, *de poenitentiis et remissionibus,* V, 38.

bishop as well as the pastor could be called the "*sacerdos proprius*," so that in making their confessions to any priest approved by the bishop the faithful were not injuring the rights of their proper pastor.[23] This unrestricted liberty was implicitly sanctioned in provincial councils held shortly after the Council of Trent.[24] In 1645 Innocent X (1644–1655) confirmed a decision of the Sacred Congregation of the Council which declared that the archbishop of Bordeaux could not forbid approved regulars from hearing the confessions of the faithful during the Paschal season.[25] Finally, on June 21, 1670, Clement X (1670–1676) formally decreed that if anyone made his confession during the Paschal season to any approved religious he satisfactorily fulfilled the requirements of the decree *Omnis utriusque sexus* as far as the Easter Confession was concerned.[26] Thus the famous decree of the IV General Council of the Lateran, which for centuries had been a bulwark for the pastor's rights relative to the annual confession of his subjects, suffered derogation, first from contrary custom and jurisprudence, and finally from statute law.[27]

The provisions of the decree *Omnis utriusque sexus* with particular reference to the Paschal communion remained in vigor however. Parishioners were bound to receive Holy Communion during Easter time in their parish church.[28] Except for this

---

[23] Benedictus XIV, *De Synodo Diocesana* (2 vols., Romae, 1806), Lib. XI, c. 14, nn. 1–6; J. B. Sägmüller, *Lehrbuch des katholischen Kirchenrechts,* 3. ed. (2 vols., Freiburg im Breisgau: Herder, 1914), II, 50–51.

[24] Conc. Rotomagense (1581), c. 37—Mansi, XXXIV, 650; Conc. Cameracense (1586), Tit. 8, c. 9—Mansi, XXXIV, 1237.

[25] Const. "*Exponi vobis*" 7 febr., 1645—*Bull. Rom.,* XV, 362.

[26] Const. "*Superna*"—*Bull. Rom.,* XVIII, 55.

[27] As late as the nineteenth century, according to Bouix, the decree "*Omnis utriusque sexus*" was still law, as far as certain pastors in France were concerned: "Non desunt enim adhuc hodie parochi in Gallia, qui parochianos suos quotannis, etiam e suggestu, monere peragant de praetensa illa obligatione proprio parocho, tum in paschate tum in mortis articulo confitendi; quique licentiam impertiantur aliis ab Episcopo approbatis confessariis (quasi haec eorum licentia necessaria foret) confessiones illas faciendi"—*Tractatus de Episcopo* (2 vols. in 1, 2. ed., Paris, 1873), II, pars quinta, c. 29, n. 6.

[28] S. C. C., *Ferrarien.,* 15 dec. 1703, 12 ian. 1704—*Fontes,* n. 3011; *Mediolanen.,* 22 iun., 24 aug., 1715—*Fontes,* n. 3147; P. Gasparri, *Tractatus*

restriction, parishioners were free to receive Holy Communion in churches and oratories of religious or in other parish churches. The parochial rights regarding the administration of Holy Viaticum and of extreme unction remained substantially intact down through the centuries to the Code. Not infrequently the pastor's right to confer the last sacraments on the canons of the cathedral chapter who resided within his territory was challenged by the chapter; the Holy See, however, was constant in upholding this parochial prerogative.[29]

The matrimonial discipline enacted in the Council of Trent required simply that a marriage be contracted before the parish priest ("*coram parocho*"), without specifying whether it meant any pastor in general or the proper pastor in particular.[30] The latter interpretation was universally adopted in jurisprudence. At an early time it received official approbation in authentic declarations of the Holy See.[31] Because of the difficulty in ascertaining who was the "*parochus proprius*," it happened very often that confusion and doubt resulted, with consequent doubt of the validity of the marriage. Accordingly in 1907 the law was amended by the decree "*Ne temere*," which simplified the rule for valid assistance at marriage.[32] Thenceforth it was the presence of the local pastor, rather than that of the proper pastor, that stood as a requisite for validity in the act of assistance at marriage. The new decree also abrogated the penalty of suspension for illegal assistance on the part of pastors, but empowered the local ordinary to punish any transgression of the law in proportion to the seriousness of the violation.[33]

Canonicus De Sanctissima Eucharistia (2 vols., Parisiis, 1897), II, cap. 11, art. 1, nn. 1076–1078.

29 S. C. C., *Mantuana*, 16 mart. 1680—*Fontes*, n. 2854; *Tiburtina*, 12 maii 1885—*Fontes*, n. 2886; *Tolentinaten.*, 11 sept. 1694—*Fontes*, n. 2944; *Novarien.*, 27 aug. 1695—*Fontes*, n. 2950; *Narnien.*, 26 sept. 1699—*Fontes*, n. 2971.

30 Sess. XXIV, *de ref.*, c. 1.

31 Const. "*Exponi Nobis*," 14 aug. 1627—*Bull. Rom.*, XIII, 591; Const. "*Paucis abhinc*," 19 mart. 1758—*Fontes*, n. 447.

32 S. C. C., 2 aug. 1907—*Fontes*, n. 4340.

33 *Ibid.*, art. X.

Article 3. *Parochial Functions*

Section 1. ORIGIN OF THE CONCEPT

In the period immediately following the Council of Trent there appeared for the first time the concept of a *parochial function* as something specifically distinct from a parochial right. Neither in any of the ancient and medieval canonical collections, nor in the commentaries of the pre-Tridentine glossators can the term "*parochial function*" (*functio parochialis*) be found. For referring to the prerogatives acquired by pastors either through custom or written law, the term "*ius parochiale*" was exclusively used. Then suddenly, in the authentic responses of the Sacred Congregations and in the canonical commentaries of the early seventeenth century, there is found mention of certain "*functiones parochiales*" side by side with the venerable "*iura parochialia*" of long standing.[34]

Probably the greatest contributing factor to the development of the new concept of parochial functions may be found in the rise of the confraternities from the thirteenth to the fifteenth centuries. These confraternities were voluntary associations of men and women, modelled to a great extent on the mendicant orders. By their preaching and example, the friars had inspired many of the laity with the desire to imitate them as far as their state of life permitted. For the sake of satisfying this need, the Third Orders were organized upon the general pattern of the great First Orders.[35] Under the stimulating influence of the vigorous apostolic spirit of the regulars, other pious associations sprang up in great numbers, especially in Italy and France, for the purpose of engaging in works of charity as well as of procuring the sanctification of its members.

Another cause of the development of confraternities is found in the medieval guilds. Permeated by the benign influence of the

---

[34] The term "*functiones parochiales*" was not universally adopted by the post-Tridentine authors. The name "*munia parochialia*" is sometimes found, as well as "*functiones ecclesiasticae*" or "*functiones privative parochi.*" Thus there was betokened the uncertainty which a lack of uniformity so often implies.

[35] Cf. A. Tachy, *Traité des Confreries et des Ouvres Pies* (2. ed., Langres, 1898), p. 25.

Church, these associations of merchants and tradesmen never lost sight of their spiritual obligations. The guild employed its resources in fostering works of charity and religion, and endeavored to further the spiritual as well as the temporal welfare of its members. In the course of time many of the guilds devoted themselves exclusively to religious ends, and lost entirely their economic character.[36]

By the sixteenth century there existed a vast network of confraternities. Their rapid increase impelled Pope Clement VIII (1592–1605) in 1604 to enact definite norms according to which the erection of confraternities was to be regulated.[37]

In their religious activities the confraternities came more and more into conflict with the pastor. Each confraternity had its own chapel in the parish church; many even possessed their own churches within the parish limits, which were administered by their own chaplains, and in which the members assisted at Holy Mass and carried out their special religious exercises. Processions were held on the feast days of patron saints and on other solemn feasts; on Sundays and other days of obligation special devotions were held in their church or chapel. Funerals of members were often held from the oratory of the confraternity, and there Requiem Masses were offered for the repose of their souls.[38] Under these circumstances one can readily perceive how conflicts could easily arise between pastors and confraternities.[39] It was from the settlement of these disputes that the distinction between parochial rights and parochial functions derived its origin.

The first known author to treat of parochial functions as well as parochial rights was Augustinus Barbosa (1589–1649).[40] Barbosa, writing around the year 1635, stated:

---

[36] Van Espen, *Ius Ecclesiasticum Universum*, Pars II, sect. 4, tit. 6, cap. 6.

[37] Const. "*Quaecumque*," 7 dec. 1604—*Fontes*, n. 192; *Bull. Rom.*, XI, 138–143.

[38] Cf. Tachy, *op. cit.*, pp. 27–31.

[39] Cf. Benedictus XIV, *Institutiones Ecclesiasticae* (Prati, 1844), Inst. CV, cap. 3, n. 91.

[40] *Summa Apostolicarum Decisionum extra Jus Commune Vagantium* (Lugduni, 1645), and *De Officio et Potestate Parochi Descriptio* (Romae, 1774).

> "Functions parochiales sunt illae quae a proprio Parocho fiunt, et quibus capellarum seu quorumvis beneficiorum simplicium Rectores, Sacristae et Capellani se intromittere nequeunt, sed tale officium ad ipsum tantum Parochum spectet."[41]

He explicitly asserted that such functions could not be included under the concept of parochial rights, but offered no specific reason for his assertion.[42] The following are the parochial functions enumerated by Barbosa:

(a) To bless the Baptismal Font;
(b) To carry the Blessed Sacrament;
(c) To celebrate Mass on Holy Thursday and Holy Saturday;
(d) To bless and distribute candles on the Feast of the Purification of the Blessed Virgin;
(e) To bless ashes on Ash Wednesday and Palms on Palm Sunday;
(f) To bless homes on Holy Saturday;
(g) To conduct processions within the parish limits.

One may readily perceive that the functions listed are of a liturgical nature, that is, they are more directly concerned with the divine cult than with the pastoral care of souls, as are the parochial rights. It is certain that pastors had performed these functions in the preceding centuries, but never were they regarded as pertaining exclusively to their office.[43] It was mainly with the development of confraternities that the nature of the functions called for a more thorough investigation.

Several decrees, especially of the Sacred Congregation of Rites, are pointed to by Barbosa as the sources for his list of parochial functions. The earliest of these decrees is dated May 18, 1602, and declared, according to Barbosa, that the carrying of the Blessed Sacrament, as well as the celebration of Mass on Holy Thursday and on Holy Saturday, was to be numbered among the parochial functions, which functions did not pertain to simple

[41] *De Officio et Potestate Parochi Descriptio,* Pars I, cap. 12, n. 1.

[42] *Ibid.*, n. 16.

[43] Cf. Burchard of Worms, *Decretorum Libri Viginti,* Lib. II, cap. 89—*MPL,* CXL, 641.

chaplains, but to proper pastors who had the care of souls.[44] From this decree it may validly be inferred that certain rectors of oratories or chaplains of confraternities had assumed the function of carrying the Blessed Sacrament, either in processions or to the sick.

Another decree referred to by Barbosa was addressed to Seville, and was dated February 26, 1628.[45] In order to put an end to the difficulties arising daily over the processions conducted by regulars as well as by confraternities in the churches of regulars, the Sacred Congregation of Rites decided that thenceforth the processions were to be confined to the cloister of the church, if the church had a cloister; if not, the procession could be led outside the church, but had to remain close to the walls, under no circumstances leaving the vicinity of the church without the permission of the pastor. In a later decree the same rules were reiterated by the Sacred Congrgation.[46] An exception previously granted in favor of the Dominicans of Pesaro, permitting them to conduct their traditional procession through the streets of the city on the Sunday within the Octave of Corpus Christi, was not prejudiced by these later decrees.[47]

---

[44] "Sanctissimi Sacramenti delationes et celebrationes Missarum Feriae quintae in Coena Domini, et Sabbati Sancti inter functiones parochiales conumerantur, et propterea tale munus non spectat ad Capellanos, sive Sacristas Ecclesiarum, sed ad proprium Parochum, seu Rectorem, animarum curam habentem, in Ecclesia institutum, ita declaravit S. Rituum Congr. sub die 18 Maii 1602."—*De Officio et Potestate Parochi Descriptio,* Pars I, cap. XII, n. 3; cf. also cap. XI, n. 50. This decree is not contained in any known collection, hence the statement of Barbosa must be taken at its face value. There is however a strikingly similar decree recorded in Monacelli, *Formularium Legale Practicum Fori Ecclesiastici* (3. ed., 4 vols. in 3, Romae, 1844), II, tit. 13, formul. 1, n. 57. According to Monacelli († 1715) it was addressed to Naples by the Sacred Congregation on May 17, 1602. The text reproduced by Monacelli "ex regestro secretariae deprompta," mentioned other functions, including the blessing of ashes, candles, palms and the baptismal font.

[45] S. R. C., *Hispalen.—Decreta Authentica Congregationis Sacrorum Rituum ex actis eiusdem collecta cura et studio Aloisii Gardellini* (3. ed., 5 vols., Romae, 1856–1879), n. 723; henceforth this work will be referred to as *DAG.*

[46] S. R. C., *Limana,* 15 dec. 1632—*DAG,* n. 970.

[47] Cf. S. R. C., *Pisauren.,* 14 nov. 1615—*Decreta Authentica Congrega-*

According to Barbosa, the same Sacred Congregation, in a response dated March 5, 1633, addressed to Alatri, declared that the blessing of candlles, of ashes, of palms, and other similar blessings were to be numbered among the parochial functions.[48] Concerning the blessing of homes on Holy Saturday, the same author pointed to two decrees of the Sacred Congregation of the Council. The first, of November 23, 1916, declared that regulars could not bless homes on Holy Saturday, since they could not exercise this function outside their own house. The second, of July 4, 1620, stated that regulars could not bless homes in Holy Week, since this was the function of the pastor.[49]

The list of parochial functions as found in Barbosa was substantially restated by Pirhing (1606–1679), but with one addition: the function of preaching in the parochial church.[50] Engel (1634–1674), on the other hand, was more conservative. He limited the parochial rights (he made no distinction between rights and functions) to the traditional enumeration, including the right to possess a baptismal font and a cemetery.[51] Reiffenstuel (1642–1703) was another who disregarded the new distinction between parochial rights and functions. He too accorded to the pastor simply the rights of long standing, which had reached their full development at the Council of Trent.[52]

Section 2. THE DECREE OF 1704

At the beginning of the eighteenth century the question of parochial functions was hopelessly tangled in a welter of confusion

---

tionis Sacrorum Rituum (6 vols., Romae: Ex Typographia Polyglotta, 1898–1927), n. 336 (hereafter referred to as *DA*). Cf. also S. R. C., *Matheranen.*, 30 apr., 1632—*DA*, n. 590.

[48] *Summa Apostolicarum Decisionum extra Jus Commune Vagantium,* CCCXCI, n. 5; *De Officio et Potestate Parochi Descriptio,* Pars I, cap. 12, n. 4.

[49] *De Officio et Potestate Parochi Descriptio, ibid.*, n. 12.

[50] *Ius Canonicum Nova Methodo Explicatum,* Lib. I, tit. 31, n. 154.

[51] *Collegium Universi Iuris Canonici* (ed. nona; post omnes alias recognita et locupleta; cui nunc primum adjectae sunt annotationes Caspari Barthel, Beneventi, 1760), Lib. III, tit. 29, cap. 1, n. 5.

[52] *Ius Canonicum Universum* (5 vols. in 6, Romae, 1831–1834), Lib. III, tit. 29, n. 9.

arising from conflicting decrees of the various Sacred Congregations and contradictory opinions of the authors. Disputes multiplied between pastors and confraternities.[53] Pastors claimed exclusive priority over certain ecclesiastical functions performed in the churches of confraternities; the confraternities on the other hand insisted that such functions were not reserved to pastors. Each side could point to some responses or some authors in support of its position. In order to settle these controversies once for all, the Sacred Congregation of Rites issued a long series of responses on January 12, 1704, in which the status of a number of the more common ecclesiastical functions was authoritatively determined.[54]

An accurate picture of the situation which existed at the time may be drawn from the brief submitted by Cardinal Colloredo preparatory to the issuance of the responses by the Sacred Congregation.[55] When on February 22, 1699, so Colloredo reported, a dispute between a pastor and a confraternity of Gubbio was referred to the Sacred Congregation, and both parties advanced a number of decrees which apparently supported their contention, the Sacred Congregation deferred decision until all the decrees could be gathered together in order that a study might be made of the principles underlying them. On August 22, 1699, the case was re-opened, but the Sacred Congregation again postponed the decision until a further examination of the decrees of other Con-

---

[53] Disputes also existed between pastors and regulars, and among pastors themselves: S. R. C., *Savonen.*, 19 dec. 1671—*DAG*, n. 2574; *Comen.*, 10 iul. 1677—*DA*, n. 1598; *Taurinen.*, 11 ian. 1681—*DAG*, n. 2937; *Mediolanen.*, 11 mart., 1684—*DAG*, n. 3048; *Fundana*, 2 sept. 1690—*DAG*, n. 3231; *Cusentina*, 15 mart. 1698—*DAG*, n. 3462; *Salernitana*, 31 mart. 1703—*DAG*, n. 3645; *Sutrina*, 28 apr. 1703—*DAG*, n. 3650. However, particular attention is directed to the disputes with confraternities, since they supplied the main impetus to the development of parochial functions: S. R. C., *Placentina*, 28 febr. 1682—*DAG*, n. 2978; *Sulmonen.*, 22 nov. 1687—*DAG*, n. 3151; *Baren.*, 11 mart. 1690—*DA*, n. 1824; *Savonen.*, 10 iun. 1690—*DAG*, n. 3223; *Asculana*, 11 aug. 1691—*DAG*, n. 3241; *Lauden.*, 20 dec. 1692—*DAG*, n. 3298; *Senogallien.*, 25 ian. 1698—*DA*, n. 1989. The foregoing lists of references are by no means intended to be exhaustive.

[54] S. R. C., *Urbis et Orbis*, 12 ian. 1704—*Fontes*, n. 5733; *DA*, n. 2123; *DAG*, n. 3670.

[55] As reproduced by Benedict XIV, *Institutiones Ecclesiasticae*, Inst. CV, cap. 3, n. 92.

gregations could be made. Again on April 30, 1701, the matter was brought forward, despite the fact that the dispute in Gubbio had long since been settled. The consistorial advocates, Sardinius and Bottinius, were called upon to submit their opinion "*pro veritate*," after which a series of thirty-three questions was formulated for solution.

Colloredo then proceeded to set forth certain principles according to which the Sacred Congregation should be guided in its replies to the questions formulated. First he reminded the Fathers that there existed, besides the parochial rights, which for the most part concerned the utility of pastors, certain parochial functions, which were so called inasmuch as they actually pertained to pastors, or inasmuch as it was fitting that they so pertain, either in view of their very nature which associated them intimately with parochial rights, or in view of their dignity and in consequence of the close bond between pastors and the parochial office.[56]

Moreover, authors were not to be relied upon in this matter, since very few of them had accurately treated the question. If an insoluble doubt should arise, Colloredo recommended that the opinion which favored the pastors should be adopted for the sake of forestalling the danger of departing from the pristine discipline of the Church. He also reminded the Sacred Congregation how cautiously and conservatively the Holy See had conducted itself in conferring privileges on the mendicant orders. *A fortiori*, he argued, confraternities had to be dealt with even more cautiously and sparingly with regard to privileges which might undermine the rights of pastors. Finally, the practice in Rome was not to be invoked as the basis of a general law, for in Rome the dignity and the primacy of the clergy rested upon a more confirmed foundation than in ordinary dioceses, and could accordingly retain the security of its status despite the more generous grants of privileges accorded to confraternities.

---

[56] ". . . ac primum praeter iura parochialia, quae cum utilitate Parochorum plerumque coniunguntur, et de quibus Canonum Interpretes frequenter verba faciunt, munia quoque Parochialia recensentur, quae ita dicta sunt, eo quod ad Parochos reipsa pertineant, aut illis saltem conveniant, vel ob naturam munerum, quae cum iuribus Parochialibus omnino copulentur, vel ob dignitatem et coniunctionem, quam habent Parochi cum Pastorali Officio. . . ." *loc. cit.*

Coming now to an examination of the series of responses themselves, one notes that a general principle was enunciated and stressed in the first four responses. Lay confraternities erected either in public churches or in public or in private oratories which, although situated within the limits of the parish, had no connection with it could carry out all non-parochial ecclesiastical functions without any dependence upon the consent of the pastor; those churches or oratories which were dependent upon a parochial church were subject to the authority of the pastor in their activities.

Then an extensive list of ecclesiastical functions was reviewed for the sake of determining which of them were strict parochial rights and which were not.[57] Thus the blessing and distribution of candles, ashes and palms were judged to be not strictly parochial rights.[58] To the question whether the blessing of women after childbirth, the blessings of the baptismal font, of fire, of seed, of eggs and of similar objects were strict parochial rights, the Sacred Congregation replied: " Negative, sed benedictiones mulierum et fontis baptismalis fieri debere a parochis." [59] In other words, the blessings of women after childbirth and of the baptismal font were declared to be parochial functions, since they pertained to the pastor, though not as strict parochial rights.

What about all the functions of Holy Week? The Sacred Congregation replied that not all may be classed as parochial rights, although the celebration of Mass on Holy Thursday pertains to pastors (i.e. as a parochial function). Regarding processions, the

---

[57] The division is made by the Sacred Congregation between "*iura mere parochialia*," or the strict rights of pastors, and "*functiones ecclesiasticae non parochiales*." The parochial functions were not explicitly mentioned, but they were indicated indirectly.

[58] *Ibid.*, ad 5.

[59] *Ibid.*, ad 6. The text of *Fontes* (n. 5733) and *DA* (n. 2123) reads simply: "benedictionem fontis baptismalis fieri debere a parochis." But this seems to be incorrect, since the copy of the response given by *DAG* (n. 3670), by Barbosa-Giraldi (*op. cit.*, Pars I, cap. 12, additio ad n. 16), by Benedict XIV (*op. cit.*, Inst. CV, cap. 3, n. 93), by Monacelli (*op. cit.*, II, tit. 13, formul. 1, n. 46) and by Ferraris (*Prompta Bibliotheca Canonica Iuridica, Moralis, Theologica, necnon Ascetica, Polemica, Rubricistica, Historica* (ed. noviss., 9 vols., Romae, 1885-1899), s.v. *Confraternitas*, art. 2, n. 5) reads as above quoted. (The work of Ferraris will hereafter be cited *Bibliotheca*).

responses substantially re-affirmed the regulations set forth in the decree of 1628.[60] The "exempt" confraternities could conduct processions, but not beyond the immediate vicinity of their churches, unless the permission of the bishop had been obtained.[61] In this fashion many other ecclesiastical functions were catalogued in successive responses. Those which were classified as neither strict parochial rights nor as pertaining to the pastor in the nature of parochial functions could be carried out licitly by the "exempt" confraternities in their own churches and oratories.

As a result of these authentic responses, which were approved by Pope Clement XI (1700–1721) on January 12, 1704, it was authoritatively recognized that there pertained to pastors, besides parochial rights, certain other prerogatives which authors referred to as parochial functions. The parochial rights had undergone no substantial changes since the Council of Trent, except the erstwhile right to have one's parishioners assist at Mass in the parochial church on Sundays and holydays, which right in the course of time had lost its juridic force. The parochial functions, according to the decree of 1704, consisted in the blessing of women after childbirth, the celebration of Mass on Holy Thursday, and the blessing of the baptismal font on Holy Saturday. Other parochial functions not explicitly declared in the decree of 1704, but based on previous decrees of the same Sacred Congregation, were the conducting of processions within the parish limits,[62] and the celebration of Mass together with the blessing of homes on Holy Saturday.[63]

Many authors maintained that the decree of 1704 was too liberal toward the confraternities, and insisted that, although many of the listed ecclesiastical functions were not strict parochial rights, they were nevertheless parochial in their nature and pertained to pastors only.[64] Schmalzgrueber (1663–1735), who wrote after 1704,

[60] S. R. C., *Hispalen.*, 26 febr. 1628—*DAG,* n. 723.

[61] S. R. C., *Urbis et Orbis,* 12 ian. 1704, ad n. 22—*Fontes,* n. 5733; *DA,* n. 2123; *DAG,* n. 3670.

[62] S. R. C., *Hispalen.*, 26 febr. 1628—*DAG,* n. 723.

[63] S. R. C., *Neapolitana,* 17 [?] maii 1602, as reproduced by Monacelli in his *Formularium Legale Practicum Fori Ecclesiastici,* II, tit. 13, formul. 1, n. 57.

[64] Cf. Benedictus XIV, *Institutiones Ecclesiasticae,* Inst. CV, cap. 4, n. 102.

evidently held such an opinion. Though he made no distinction between parochial rights and functions, yet in his list of parochial rights (*iura parochialia*) he included the blessings of ashes, of palms and of candles, as well as the parochial functions mentioned in the decree of 1704.[65] Schmalzgrueber also included the functions of preaching the word of God, of receiving tithes, and of announcing not only the banns of marriage but also the feast days, the vigils, the jubilees and the indulgences.[66]

Monacelli († 1715), on the other hand, made explicit reference to the responses of 1704; in fact he reproduced the text in its entirety.[67] Yet in his list of parochial functions he included the blessing of palms, of ashes, and of candles, and the exposition of the Blessed Sacrament, notwithstanding the responses of the Sacred Congregation to the contrary.[68] Monacelli justified this apparent contradiction of the decree on two counts. He maintained first of all that, even though these functions were not strict parochial rights, they nonetheless pertained to pastors by reason of their intimate connection with the parochial office and the care of souls.[69] Then he appealed to the earlier decrees whose authority, so he declared, had not been abrogated by the decree of 1704. Monacelli's definition of parochial functions reveals a striking resemblance to that given by Colloredo: ". . . ad parochum pertinent, vel propter affinitatem, connexionem et dependentiam quam habent a iuribus mere parochialibus, vel ratione officii pastoralis quo vices gerit episcopi in regimine curae animarum. . . ." [70]

Benedict XIV (Prosper Lambertini, 1675–1758), on the other hand, held that the responses of 1704 constituted the final decision in the matter of ecclesiastical functions. Accordingly those matters which had been expressly declared not to be strict parochial rights or parochial functions could be freely exercised by churches and oratories which were not subsidiary to any parochial church.[71]

---

[65] *Ius Ecclesiasticum Universum*, Lib. III, tit. 29, n. 12.

[66] *Ibid.*, nn. 11, 12.

[67] *Formularium Legale Practicum Fori Ecclesiastici*, II, tit. 13, formul. 1, n. 46.

[68] *Ibid.*, n. 54.

[69] *Ibid.*, n. 57.

[70] *Ibid.*, n. 54; cf. *supra*, footnote 56 for the text of Colloredo.

[71] ". . . sed haec utilitas (Decreti 1704) minime sequeretur, nec ullum

De Bonis († after 1761) maintained the same opinion.[72] Ferraris († ca. 1763) made no distinction between parochial rights and functions, but simply referred the reader to the *Institutiones Ecclesiasticae* of Benedict XIV for a more detailed study of the question.[73] De Fargna († after 1719) adopted the division made by the Sacred Congregation of Rites between strictly parochial functions and functions that were not strictly parochial.[74] De Fargna departed from the text of the responses, however, in labelling the blessing of the baptismal font, the blessing of women after childbirth, and all the functions of Holy Week an non-parochial functions which could be exercised by any chaplain or rector.[75] The Cassinese Editors incorporated almost verbatim the teaching of De Fargna in their appendix to the *Prompta Bibliotheca* of Ferraris.[76]

Article 4. *The Fusion of Parochial Rights and Functions*

The evolution of parochial functions did not completely end with the decree of 1704. A response of the Sacred Congregation of the Council on May 19 and June 9, 1708, is reported by Giraldi of St. Cajetan (1692–1775) in his additions to Barbosa's work, *De Officio et Potestate Parochi Descriptio.* The response permitted the Carmelites of Aix-la-Chapelle to impart the blessing after childbirth in their own church.[77] On December 3, 1718, the same Sacred Congregation flatly declared that the right to bless women after childbirth did not belong exclusively to the pastor.[78]

---

finem haberent dissidia, si postquam Sac. Congregatio constituit aliquid non esse de juribus Parochialibus, illud peragendum a Capellanis sodalitatum non concederetur"—*Institutiones Ecclesiasticae,* Inst. CV, cap. 6, n. 102.

[72] *De Oratoriis Publicis* (Mediolani, 1761), cap. 7, n. 96.

[73] *Bibliotheca,* s.v. *Confraternitas,* art. 2, n. 6; s.v. *Parochia,* n. 22.

[74] *Commentaria in Singulos Canones de Jure Patronatus* (3 vols., Montisfalisci: Romae, 1717–1719), Pars I, c. 4, casus 9, n. 1.

[75] *Ibid.,* nn. 6, 9.

[76] S.v. *Confraternitas,* art. 4, n. 20.

[77] Pars I, cap. 12, n. 12, *additio.*

[78] S. C. C., *Derthonen.,* 3 dec. 1718—*Thesaurus Resolutionum Sacrae Congregationis Concilii* (167 vols., Romae, 1718–1908), I, 132 (henceforth referred to as *Thesaurus*).

This statement was further amplified in a subsequent response, in which the Sacred Congregation declared that those who wished to receive the blessing after childbirth were free to request it in whatever church they pleased.[79]

More than a century after the decree of 1704 the question of parochial functions still constituted a knotty problem for canonists, as Bouix (1808–1870) confessed in his treatise on pastors.[80] The precise nature of parochial functions was still as much a mystery then as it was at the beginning of the eighteenth century, for Bouix could find no better definition than that which Colloredo proposed, when he characterized parochial functions as being essentially honorary. The responses of 1704 were still being relied upon as giving the only definite norms in the matter.[81] Bouix noted that the Sacred Congregation of the Council had denied that the blessing of women after childbirth was a parochial function, but he was uncertain whether or not it abrogated the decree of 1704 in this respect.[82]

Towards the end of the nineteenth century a trend began among authors to conglomerate all parochial prerogatives in one group, thereby eliminating any distinction between rights and functions. Santi (1830–1885) strove for a clearer understanding by grouping all the parochial rights and functions under the title "*munera parochorum.*" He then divided them according to their relation either to the sacraments or to the sacramentals.[83] Santi interpreted the decree of 1704 as having removed the blessing of women after childbirth and the blessing of the baptismal font from the category

---

[79] S. C. C., *Derthonen.*, 7 dec. 1720—*Thesaurus*, I, 399.

[80] "Nulla fere materia tot litibus et dubiis ortum dedit quam ea, de qua nunc nobis agendum est, jura et munia parochorum propria respiciens. . . ." *Tractatus de Parocho*, Pars IV, cap. 1, p. 436.

[81] Cf. J. Soglia, *Institutiones Juris Privati Ecclesiastici* (2. ed., Parisiis, 1842), Lib. I, cap. 3, n. 27; S. Aichner, *Compendium Juris Ecclesiastici* (6. ed., Brixinae, 1887), n. 127, 429–443.

[82] *Op. cit.*, Pars IV, cap. 11, sect. 41, p. 501.

[83] *Praelectiones Juris Canonici* (editio quarta emendata et recentissimis decretis accommodata cura Martini Leitner, 5 vols., Ratisbonae, Romae, Neo Eboraci et Cincinnati, 1903–1905), Lib. III, tit. 29, n. 9.

of parochial rights, and placed them among the parochial obligations.[84]

Wernz (1842–1914), like Santi, eliminated the twofold classification of parochial rights and parochial functions, and treated only of parochial rights in the strict sense. These he described as pertaining to the care of souls, and as exercisable only by the pastor, in his own territory, with reference to his own subjects.[85] He grouped these rights under five distinct headings, in which parochial functions are mingled indiscriminately with parochial rights. Thus the blessing of the baptismal font is placed in the first heading along with the right of pastors to baptize their subjects. Under the second heading Wernz listed the celebration of Mass on Holy Thursday, another parochial function. Certain blessings are grouped under the fifth heading, without explicit mention of any one in particular.[86]

The fusion of rights and functions was completed in the legislation of the Code of Canon Law (1918).[87]. There, under the title "Functions reserved to the pastor" (*functiones parocho reservatae*), rights and functions are listed indiscriminately, without any indication whatever that one function might differ from another in its nature. The old vexatious problem of the specific difference between parochial rights and parochial functions is happily by-passed in the new legislation.

Several striking changes are noticeable in the new law. The Easter Communion is neither implicitly nor explicitly mentioned in the new list. No longer were parishioners bound to fulfill this precept in their parish church. The right to announce the sacred ordination of his parishioners is here for the first time included among the functions reserved to the pastor.[88]

The blessing of women after childbirth, on the other hand, is

---

[84] *Ibid.*, n. 14.

[85] *Ius Decretalium* (2. ed., 6 vols., Romae et Prati, 1906–1913), II, pars 2, tit. 39, sect. 4, n. 829.

[86] *Loc. cit.* In a footnote to the fifth heading Wernz referred to the contradictory decrees concerning the blessing of women after childbirth.

[87] C. 462.

[88] *Ibid.*, n. 4.

not listed among the reserved functions; no longer can there be any doubt concerning the non-parochial character of this function. No longer, indeed, can there be any doubt concerning the functions whose exercise belongs by right to pastors. The beguiling simplicity and clarity of the list mentioned in canon 462 give no indication of the centuries of canonical and jurisprudential development that were entailed in their formation.

Part II

CANONICAL COMMENTARY

CHAPTER III

RESERVED PAROCHIAL FUNCTIONS IN GENERAL

Article 1. *The Subject of Reserved Functions*

THE reserved parochial functions enumerated in canon 462 may be divided into personal functions and impersonal functions. The personal functions (nn. 1°–5°) are those which are exercised directly for the spiritual benefit of some person or persons, for example, the administration of the sacrament of baptism or of extreme unction. The impersonal functions (nn. 6°–7°), on the other hand, have the divine cult rather than some person's spiritual welfare as their immediate end, for example, a public procession. The latter group may be said to belong to pastors in general. Most of the functions of the first group, however, require that a certain relationship exist between the pastor and those in whose favor the functions are exercised: in other words, the pastor must also be the *proper* pastor. Before proceeding to deal with the reserved functions in particular, one must, as a preliminary, establish just who comes under the concept of pastor. Furthermore, one must likewise outline the notion of a proper pastor, at least in so far as it implies a common element in relation to the functions listed in the first group. Whatever peculiarities exist will be delineated when the individual functions will be treated.

The term "pastor" is defined in the Code as a priest or a moral person to whom there has been granted in title a parish with the care of souls, to be exercised under the authority of the local ordinary.[1] However, when the pastor is a moral person (for example, a religious community), the law requires that a vicar be appointed for the actual ministrations of the pastorate for the parishioners, with all the rights and obligations of pastor.[2]

[1] Canon 451, §1.

[2] Canon 471.

According to canon 451, § 2, the following are to be regarded as equivalent to pastors, possessing all their rights and privileges:

(a) Quasi-pastors (can. 216, § 3);

(b) The actual vicar of a parish held in title by a moral person (can. 471);

(c) The substitute vicar (can. 465, §§ 4 and 5; 474; 1923, § 2);

(d) The parish administrator (can. 472, 1°; 473);

(e) The curate lawfully constituted to act as pastor when the parochial office falls vacant (can. 472, 2°);

(f) The adjutant vicar who is deputed with full powers (can. 475);

(g) The assistant vicar who for the exercise of the pastoral power has unrestricted authorization from the diocesan statutes, from the ordinary's letter of appointment, or from the commission given him by the pastor himself (can. 1412, 1°).

Rectors of seminaries hold the office of pastor in relation to all those living in the seminary, exception being made solely with reference to the sacraments of penance and matrimony.[3] Therefore all the functions reserved to pastors, except those which pertain to the sacrament of matrimony, are reserved to the rector of a seminary, and may not be performed by any priest without his express permission.[4] On the other hand, rectors of churches and the chaplains of confraternities do not hold the office of pastor, and consequently must abstain from exercising any of the functions reserved to pastors, unless an exception be made by particular law.[5]

The term "proper pastor" further adds to the notion of pastor the element of a stable, juridic relationship, existing between the pastor and the faithful living within his parish. The basis of the relationship is the domicile or quasi-domicile of the parishioner within the parish limits.[6] Parochial domicile consists in actual residence (*commoratio*) in the parish, plus

[3] Canon 1368.

[4] *Jus Pontificium* (Romae, 1921—), XVI (1936), 91.

[5] Canons 481 and 1171.

[6] Canon 94, §1.

(a) the intention of living there permanently, or

(b) a ten years' residence already completed.[7]

[7] Canon 92, §1.

Parochial quasi-domicile is acquired by actual residence, plus

(a) the intention of remaining for at least the greater part of the year, or

(b) a sojourn already protracted through the greater part of a year.[8]

It will be noted that in both domicile and quasi-domicile a *commoratio,* i.e., an actual residence or sojourn, is required.[9]

The proper pastor therefore is the pastor of the parish in which one has a domicile or a quasi-domicile.[10] The question naturally arises: what about those who have no domicile or quasi-domicile? Or about those who have a domicile or quasi-domicile in a diocese, but not in any particular parish of that diocese? The law provides for these cases by designating the pastor of the place of actual residence as their proper pastor.[11]

Since it is possible to have more than one domicile at the same time, or one domicile and at least one quasi-domicile simultaneously, it is therefore possible also to have more than one proper pastor, each of whom would have an equal right to perform those reserved functions which call for the proper pastor.[12] No general norm exists by which these overlapping rights may be adjusted, although in the particular case of the function of burial the law has prescribed a definite mode of procedure for such an eventual-

[8] Canon 92, §2.

[9] "Censetur commorari, qui domum, sive propriam sive conductam, more aliorum civium per tempus requisitum colit. Non sufficit mera residentia, etiam diuturnior, aut aedium, praediorum, officinae possessio, aut secundum leges civiles adscriptio inter municipes."—Cappello, *Summa Iuris Canonici* (3 vols., Vol. I, II, 3. ed., Romae: Universitas Gregoriana, 1938–1939), I, n. 193, p. 223 (hereafter cited as *Summa*); S. C. S. Off., *litt. encycl.,* 7 iun. 1867—*Fontes,* n. 1001.

[10] S. C. C., *Ardachaden.,* 11 iun. 1923—*The Irish Ecclesiastical Record* (Dublin, 1864—), 5. series, XXVI (1925), 552.

[11] Canon 94, §§2 and 3.

[12] Costello, *Domicile and Quasi-Domicile,* The Catholic University of American Canon Law Studies, n. 60 (Washington, D. C.: The Catholic University of America, 1930), p. 154.

ity.[13] This situation will be further explored in the succeeding study of the individual reserved functions.

Article 2. *The Signification of "nisi aliud iure caveatur"*

Under the common law, pastors are accorded their exclusive prerogatives with one important condition: "nisi aliud iure caveatur." [14] If is not therefore the intention of the legislator that these functions be so inflexibly determined as to preclude the possibility of any further legal intervention. But the precise import of the laconic phrase, "*nisi aliud iure caveatur,*" is doubtful; to what extent the common law enacted in canon 462 will permit alteration is not certain.

The crux of the problem concerns the proper understanding of the term "*ius*" as it is used in the phrase, "*nisi aliud iure caveatur.*" When it is found in the Code standing alone, not modified by any qualifying adjective, the word "*ius*" can lend itself to several varying significations. In each individual instance, the proper meaning of the word is to be deduced from the context of the canon; if the context fails to clarify the meaning, some indication must then be sought in parallel passages of the Code, if there are any, and in the end and circumstances of the law.[15]

In its most restricted sense, the word "*ius,*" as employed in the Code, signifies the common law only. This is the obvious meaning of the term in canon 103, §2.[16] In the widest sense of the term, however, "*ius*" signifies not only the common law, but particular law also, as it exists in any of its legitimate forms, whether written or unwritten. According to many authors, the word is employed in this sense in canons 172, §1, 177, §4 and 179, §1.[17]

---

[13] Canon 1216, §2.

[14] Canon 462.

[15] Canon 18.

[16] "Actus positi ex metu gravi et iniuste incusso vel ex dolo, valent, nisi aliud iure caveatur. . . ."

[17] Cf. Coronata, *Institutiones Iuris Canonici* (5 vols., Vol. I–II, 2. ed., 1939; Vol. III, 2. ed., 1941; Vol. IV, 2. ed., 1945; Vol. V, 1936, Taurini: Marietti), I, nn. 241, 252; Beste, *Introductio in Codicem* (2. ed., Collegeville, Minn.: St. John's Abbey Press, 1944), p. 58, nota 27, pp. 207, 208; Michiels, *Normae Generales Juris Canonici* (2 vols., Lublin: Universitas Catholica, 1929), I, 95; Vermeersch-Creusen, *Epitome Iuris Canonici* (3

Coming now to the interpretation of "*ius*" as it occurs in canon 462, the writer is of the opinion that the term is to be understood in its widest sense as embracing particular as well as common law. The writer's opinion is based on two arguments drawn: (a) from the status of parochial rights under pre-Code law; and (b) from the teaching of contemporary canonists.

A. *From the status of parochial functions in pre-Code legislation.* A broad interpretation of "*ius*" is regarded by the writer as being more in consonance with the concept of parochial rights manifested in traditional jurisprudence and pre-Code legislation. From the very beginning of the parochial system it has been the teaching of jurists that the bishop [18] was the proper pastor of his people, exercising direct and immediate jurisdiction in every part of his diocese. Pastors were the helpers of the bishop, and whatever rights pastors possessed were but a participation of the rights radically vested in the bishop.[19]

It is true that the Holy See occasionally found it necessary to enact legislation with respect to parochial rights which thereby curtailed, but by no means destroyed, the local ordinary's power over those same rights. Indeed, whenever the bishop's power to control the jurisdiction and rights of pastors was called in question, the Sacred Congregations unconditionally upheld the bishop,

---

vols., Vol. I, 6. ed., Romae: Dessain, 1937; Vol. II, 6. ed., 1940), I, n. 76 (hereafter cited as *Epitome*); Neuberger, *Canon 6, or the Relation of the Codex Iuris Canonici to the Preceding Legislation,* The Catholic University of America Canon Law Studies, n. 44, Washington, D. C.: The Catholic University of America, 1927), p. 46.

[18] The term "bishop" signifies the residential bishop, and, unless it is expressly stated otherwise, whatever is attributed to the bishop in relation to the reserved parochial functions may be equally applied to the other local ordinaries, including the vicar and prefect apostolic, since quasi-pastors enjoy the same rights as pastors (canon 451, §2, 1o).

[19] ". . . iura parochorum non sunt ita exaggeranda, ut potestas pastoralis ipsius Episcopi in parochiam et dioecesim videatur negari. Quare Episcopus non prohibetur, quominus etiam invitis parochis cum moderatione quadam aliis sacerdotibus functiones sacras in parochiis peragendas deleget." Wernz, *Ius Decretalium,* II, pars secunda, tit. 39, sect. 4, n. 828. Cf. Thomassinus, *Vetus et Nova Ecclesiae Disciplina,* Pars I, lib. II, c. 10, n. 10; Barbosa, *De Officio et Potestate Parochi Descriptio,* Pars II, Compendium, n. 24.

provided that there was no conflict with the prescriptions of the common law.[20]

Moreover, from the time of the Council of Trent until the promulgation of the Code, the Decree of the Sacred Congregation of Rites in 1704 was the only universal law enacted concerning parochial rights and functions.[21] It was the purpose of this law to clarify the then existing confusion in the matter, and to decide the precise nature of a number of ecclesiastical functions, yet the law was enacted with the explicit provision: " salvis tamen conventionibus et pactis . . . constitutionibus synodalibus et provincialibus. . . ." [22] Since a doubt exists whether canon 462 differs in juridic force from the old law which it supplants, it is to be presumed that the new law does not depart from the traditional legislation by excluding the possibility of further development and modification of parochial functions through the agency of diocesan or provincial law.[23]

Parochial rights are not an end in themselves. They are the means used to achieve an orderly and efficient parochial organization. Now, since the difficulties that may hamper the parochial system will not necessarily be the same everywhere, it is to be desired that the parochial functions be not rigidly fixed in one inflexible pattern. Freedom of development is needed to cope with the ever shifting circumstances of particular localities. This is not possible unless the bishop be given the power to modify, as circumstances may demand, the functions reserved to pastors.

B. *From the teaching of contemporary canonists.* Commenting upon the clause "*nisi aliud iure caveatur*" in canon 462, Cappello makes the following statement: " Hoc ius peculiare multiplex est, scil., lex fundationis, privilegium apostolicum, legitima consuetudo,

[20] " Sunt certe parochis nonnulla iura: at non ita absoluta, ut nulli sint obnoxia limitationi seu restrictioni; ipsi enim episcoporum subsunt iurisdictioni, qui eorumdem, aliorumque rectorum ecclesiarum totius dioecesis regimen moderantur."—S. C. C., *Placentina,* 6 iun. 1917—*Acta Apostolicae Sedis, Commentarium Officiale* (Romae, 1909—), IX (1917), 581 (hereafter referred to as *AAS*). Cf. also S. C. C., 14 aug. 1863, ad 3—*Fontes,* n. 4195, or *Collectanea S. Congregationis de Propaganda Fide,* I, n. 1241.

[21] Cf. *supra,* p.

[22] *DA,* n. 2123, or *Fontes,* n. 5733.

[23] Canon 6, 4o.

lex dioecesana seu statutum Episcopi, conventio inter parochos inita et a loci ordinario approbata, praescriptio debitis condicionibus vestita." [24] Coronata is also of the opinion that "*ius*" in this instance is to be understood in its widest sense.[25] Blat [26] and Chelodi [27] also accord to the term the same broad interpretation.

Since it has been established as the more probable opinion that "*ius*" in the clause "*nisi aliud iure caveatur*" includes particular law as well as common law, it follows that whatever exceptions particular law may have presented in 1918, when the Code became operative law, are not necessarily abrogated. By virtue of this explicit provision, any contrary enactment of particular law, whether it be in the form of a statute, of a custom or of a privilege, remains in vigor, *provided that it does not conflict with other prescriptions of the Code.* If, therefore, the pastors of a certain locality had succeeded in vindicating to themselves other exclusive prerogatives over and above those which are listed in canon 462 (for example, the solemn first Communion of children), these rights retain their legal force on the strength of the express concession, "*nisi aliud iure caveatur.*" On the other hand, if particular law had already enforced certain restrictions on parochial functions not mentioned in canon 462 or in the other canons of the Code, the particular law remains operative, in conjunction with canon 462, in that locality.

It follows also, as a consequence of this broad interpretation of "*ius*," that inferior legislators may continue to enact legislation governing parochial functions, either by way of derogation or amplification, provided that the particular statute does not come into conflict with the common law. It cannot be too strongly emphasized, however, that this freedom which is accorded to

---

[24] *Summa,* II, n. 507.

[25] "Dicitur in c. *nisi aliud iure caveatur;* aliud statui potest aut ipsa lege Codicis, ut pro regularibus exemptis, et pro Seminario; aut iure, statuto, consuetudine aut praescriptione alicubi vigente . . ."—*Institutiones Iuris Canonici,* I, n. 481, nota 6.

[26] *Commentarium Textus Codicis Iuris Canonici* (5 vols. in 7, Vol. II, pars 1, *De Personis,* 2. ed., Romae: Ex Typographia Pontificia in Instituto Pii X, 1923), II, pars 1, n. 509.

[27] *Ius de Personis* (3. ed., curavit P. Ciprotti, Trento: Libreria Moderna Edititrice, 1942), n. 226, e.

inferior legislators by the "*nisi*" clause must always be exercised either "*secundum Codicem*" or "*praeter Codicem,*" never "*contra Codicem.*"

Article 3. *Possible Modes of Restriction Upon Reserved Parochial Functions*

Assuming that the clause, "*nisi aliud iure caveatur,*" is to be interpreted in the widest sense, one must thereupon investigate the various modes of restriction upon parochial functions which are possible in virtue of the "*nisi*" clause. In this manner it is hoped that some estimation may be gained of the juridic force of their reservation under the new law.

The first possible mode of restriction is the common law itself. In the legislation of the Code concerning the administration of the sacraments, the bestowing of ecclesiastical burial, etc., some specific prescriptions are enacted which indirectly constitute limitations upon the rights accorded to pastors by canon 462. It is reserved to the pastor, for example, to administer the sacraments of Extreme Unction and Holy Viaticum to the faithful residing within the limits of his parish. But canon 464, §2, empowers the local ordinary, for a just cause, to withdraw from the pastor's jurisdiction a hospital or a home for the aged which lies within the parish limits, and to delegate a chaplain to attend to its spiritual necessities.[28] This and other canons of the Code which have a bearing upon parochial functions will be considered in the subsequent chapters when the individual functions will be studied in detail.

The diocesan (or provincial) statute is another possible mode of restriction upon parochial functions. By divine law the bishop is the shepherd of the souls under his care, and to this end he possesses the ordinary power of jurisdiction over his diocese. This power is to be exercised under the authority of the Roman Pontiff and subject to the prescriptions of the common law.[29] This ordinary power of the bishop is sedulously safeguarded in

[28] Cf. Prümmer, *Manuale Iuris Canonici* (6. ed., Friburgi Brisgoviae: Herder, 1933), n. 152, p. 208.

[29] Cf. Bouix, *Tractatus de Episcopo* (2. ed., Parisiis, 1873), I, c. 5, prop. 8; Wernz, *Ius Decretalium,* II, pars secunda, tit. 39, n. 828.

the Code, canon 462 furnishing a typical example. Exclusive rights should be accorded to pastors, but exclusive rights can become harmful, and therefore the bishop must be free to act if such a danger should occur.[30] For the same reason other local ordinaries as well as the bishop should possess the power to qualify the provisions of canon 462.

As it has already been stated, the diocesan statute must not conflict with any of the provisions of the common law. The bishop could not, for example, decree that solemn baptism may be administered only by the vicar general and by the rural deans of his diocese, for such a statute would be contrary to canon 738, §1. However, a diocesan statute which would curtail the right of pastors to carry out the solemn blessing of homes on Holy Saturday could hardly be regarded as contrary to the common law, since it does not conflict with any other canon of the Code, whereas its inclusion in canon 462 is conditional: "*nisi aliud iure caveatur.*" It is presumed, of course, that such a statute of the local ordinary would be motivated by a proportionately just cause.

Parochial functions may also be affected, in addition to the diocesan statutes, by other forms of particular law which might make their influence felt through the religious houses in the diocese. When a clerical religious order or a clerical religious congregation receives the permission of a local ordinary to erect a house in his diocese, the permission automatically carries with it the right to build a church or a public oratory contiguous to the house.[31] Though it be assumed that the church is not constituted a parochial church, there may nevertheless be performed in it all the sacred functions except such as are reserved to pastors.[32] The exercise of these functions pertains exclusively to the pastor within whose territory the religious house is situated. It is possible, however, for a religious house to acquire the right to perform some one or other of the reserved functions apart from the need of a permission given by the pastor. In such a case the function

---

[30] S. C. C., *Placentina*, 6 iun. 1917—*AAS*, IX (1917), 581.

[31] Canon 497, §1 and §2; cf. Schaefer, *De Religiosis ad Normam Codicis Iuris Canonici* (3. ed., Romae: S.A.L.E.R., 1940), p. 211.

[32] Canon 1171.

in question becomes divested of its reserved character as far as that particular pastor is concerned.

Legitimate custom is one way in which the right to the exercise of reserved functions may be acquired by religious houses. If an ecclesiastical law does not expressly prohibit this, a contrary usage which is reasonable and continuously exercised for forty years can grow to the juridic estate of an established custom which abrogates that law.[33] Now, canon 462 does not prohibit the formation of contrary customs in the future; therefore, a derogatory custom may arise. On the other hand, if such a particular custom was already in existence at the time when the new law became binding, it would have remained in force by virtue of the clause: "*nisi aliud iure caveatur.*" [34]

The apostolic indult is another means whereby the right to exercise reserved parochial functions could be obtained. The Pope is the supreme lawmaker and exercises direct and immediate jurisdiction throughout the entire Church. There have been many instances of such indults in the past, as has been noted in the preceding chapters. Again, the local ordinary himself may by means of a special indult grant to the religious house the faculty to perform reserved functions. Naturally the granting of such an indult would postulate the existence of a sufficient reason. In order to foster greater devotion to St. Anthony of Padua, for example, a bishop might permit the Franciscans to conduct a public procession on the feast day of the saint, even though such a function is reserved by the Code to pastors.

---

[33] Canons 25 and 27; S. C. C., *Pontiscurvi,* 30 iun. 1906—*Acta Sanctae Sedis* (41 vols., Romae, 1865-1908), XXXIX (1906), 461-467; S. R. R., *Segusina, Iuris Canendi Missas Adventicias,* 12 iul. 1913, coram R. P. D. Antonio Perathoner—*AAS,* V (1913), 525.

[34] Canon 462; cf. Michiels, *Normae Generales Juris Canonici,* I, 82.

CHAPTER IV

RESERVED FUNCTIONS IN THE ADMINISTRATION OF THE SACRAMENTS

Article 1. *Baptism*

THE sacrament of baptism can be administered in either of two forms: private or solemn. The private form is brief, comprising only those elements which are necessary for the valid administration of the sacrament. Under ordinary circumstances private baptism is licit only when the local ordinary permits it in the case of heretics who as adults are baptized conditionally.[1] With this exception, private baptism may be employed only in a case of necessity, namely, in danger of death or in circumstances which would render the administration of solemn baptism impossible.[2] Since baptism is the gateway to the sacraments and absolutely necessary for one's eternal salvation, it may be administered in its private form by all persons alike, provided that they have the proper intention.[3] The Church, like a loving mother, does all she can to make the sacrament of spiritual regeneration most accessible to souls.

Outside the case of necessity, however, baptism is not to be administered except in the solemn form. Since the earliest centuries the Church has endeavored to emphasize and enhance the importance and dignity of this sacrament by enshrining it within a sacred setting of solemn rites and of ceremonies full of beauty in their simplicity and symbolism. It is under this form, more befitting to the sacred character of the sacrament and more bene-

---

1 Canon 759, §2.

2 "Casus necessitatis est in solo periculo mortis: non autem si sacerdos ob distantiam, intemperiem vel infirmitatem haberi non possit nisi post diuturnum tempus. Sufficit autem *probabile* periculum mortis, imo fundatus timor . . ."—Merkelbach, *Summa Theologiae Moralis* (3. ed., 3 vols., Parisiis: Desclée, de Brouwer et Cie, 1939), III, n. 139.

3 Canon 742, §1; Rituale Romanum, Tit. 2, c. 1, *de sacr. bapt.*, n. 16.

ficial spiritually to the one being baptized, that baptism is normally to be administered.[4] It is under this form, too, that the administration of baptism is reserved exclusively to the pastors, or more precisely to the proper pastor.[5]

The objection may immediately be raised that before baptism no one is subject to the purely ecclesiastical laws of the Church.[6] It would seem, therefore, that a pastor could not claim anyone as his subject before baptism, and, vice versa, before baptism no one could point to any pastor as his proper pastor.[7] This objection one may answer by making a distinction between direct and indirect subjection to ecclesiastical law. It is true that before baptism no one is directly bound by the law of the Church. But a nonsubject can be bound indirectly, as for example in his contracting of marriage with one who is subject to the law. So, in the case of baptism, it is the pastors who are directly bound by the ecclesiastical discipline, and in the case of the children of Catholic parents it is the latter who are thus bound; the person to be baptized is bound only indirectly.[8] Over and above this indirect necessary subjection to the Church discipline, it may be presumed that an adult candidate for baptism would be readily disposed to subject himself voluntarily to the regulations governing the reception of the sacrament.

Concerning the supplying of ceremonies subsequent to private baptism, the law is silent and canonists are not unanimous in conceding this function to the exclusive competence of the proper pastor. Vermeersch-Creusen and Bouscaren-Ellis maintain that

---

[4] Canon 755, §1; S. C. de Prop. Fide, instr., 30 aug. 1775: ". . . non exiguis spiritualibus bonis, quae ex adhibitis . . . sacris caeremoniis . . . derivantur."—*Fontes,* n. 4569.

[5] Canons 462, 1°, and 738, §1. Cf. Schaefer, *Die Kirchenämter nach dem Codex Iuris Canonici,* II Band, Pfarrer und Pfarrvikare (Erste und zweite Auflage, Münster i.W.: Verlag der Aschendorffen Verlagsbuchhandlung, 1922), p. 27.

[6] Canon 12.

[7] Cf. Augustine, *A Commentary on the New Code of Canon Law* (8 vols., Vol. IV, 6. ed., St. Louis: Herder, 1931), IV, 41 (hereafter cited *Commentary*).

[8] Cf. Waldron, *The Minister of Baptism,* p. 101.

it belongs to the proper pastor to supply the ceremonies.[9] Cappello is hesitant, and he seems ready to concede this to be a reserved function only when it takes place at the font of the parish church.[10]

Section 1. THE BAPTISM OF THOSE HAVING A DOMICILE OR A QUASI-DOMICILE WITHIN THE PARISH

Three problems concerning the choice of the proper pastor immediately present themselves for consideration. The first problem may well arise in the event of a plurality of domiciles. As it has already been noted, a person is capable of possessing more than one domicile simultaneously, and of having consequently more than one proper pastor, so that each of these pastors obtains equal competence for the conferring of the baptism. Concerning such an eventuality the Code is silent. Freedom of choice is thereby accorded to the candidate, or to his parents or guardian, concerning the minister and place of baptism.[11] The opinion has been expressed that this situation may well be the subject of a particular statute defining which of the several proper pastors would have the preferred right to baptize.[12] Beste, on the other hand, maintains that such a statute would be contrary to the spirit, if not also the letter, of the common law, which sedulously refrains from curtailing the just right of any proper pastor.[13] It is the opinion of the writer that, although such a statute could be justified as a further specification of the more general norm of the Code, still the need for such specification can hardly be said to exist in this case, and the utility of the statute could well be questioned.

Another problem arising from a plurality of domiciles concerns

---

[9] *Epitome,* II, n. 22; Bouscaren-Ellis, *Canon Law, A Text and Commentary* (Milwaukee: Bruce, 1946), p. 203.

[10] *Summa,* II, n. 508, p. 49.

[11] Maroto, *Institutiones Iuris Canonici* (2 vols., Vol. I, 3. ed., 1921; Vol. II, 1919, Romae: Apud Commentarium pro Religiosis), I, n. 415, nota 1; Coronata, *Institutiones Iuris Canonici,* I, n. 124, p. 127.

[12] Claeys Boúúaert-Simenon, *Manuale Juris Canonici* (3 vols., Vols. I and III, 3. ed., Vol. II, 1. ed., Gandae et Leodii: Dessain, 1930–1931), II, n. 19; Michiels, *Principia Generalia de Personis in Ecclesia* (Lublin: Universitas Catholica, 1932), pp. 169–172.

[13] *Introduction in Codicem,* p. 140.

the baptism of infants whose parents possess both a domicile and a quasi-domicile. According to the law, a minor retains the domicile of the person to whom he is subject, and this constitutes a necessary or legal domicile for the child.[14] However, if the father possess both a domicile and a quasi-domicile, canonists disagree as to whether or not the child shares in the necessary or legal quasi-domicile also.[15] The affirmative opinion seems sufficiently probable to be acted upon. Hence, until there is had an authoritative declaration to the contrary, the pastor of the quasi-domicile may licitly baptize the child, if the father should choose him, rather than the pastor of his domicile, to be the minister of the sacrament.

A further problem, which is accorded a surprisingly exhaustive treatment by many authors, concerns the determination of the proper pastor of those whose house is situated on the boundary between two parishes. In such a case it is a general principle of jurisprudence that the location of the main entrance is to be the deciding factor, and thus that pastor is the proper pastor in whose territory the main entrance of the house is situated.[16]

Once the problem of ascertaining the proper pastor is settled, little difficulty remains in the baptism of those subjects who have a domicile or a quasi-domicile within the parish. Concerning the baptism of adults, however, it is necessary to note that the law

[14] Canon 93, §1.

[15] Among the authors maintaining that the Code has entirely eliminated the concept of a necessary quasi-domicile may be cited: Vermeersch-Creusen, *Epitome,* I, n. 185; De Meester, *Juris Canonici et Juris Canonico-Civilis Compendium* (nova editio, 3 vols. in 4, Brugis, 1921–1928), I, n. 318, nota 7; Toso, *Ad Codicem Iuris Canonici . . . Commentaria Minora* (5 vols., Romae: Marietti, 1920–1927), II, 21; Ojetti, *Commentarium in Codicem Iuris Canonici* (4 vols., Romae: Universitas Gregoriana, 1927–1931), II, 50, nota 40. Opposed to this view are Wernz-Vidal, *Ius Canonicum* (7 vols. in 8, Vol. II, 2. ed., 1928, Romae: Universitas Gregoriana), II, n. 12; Claeys Boúúaert-Simenon, *Manuale Juris Canonici,* I, n. 245; Michiels, *Principia Generalia de Personis in Ecclesia,* pp. 150–152; Chelodi, *Ius de Personis,* n. 92; Cappello, *Summa,* I, n. 195.

[16] Cappello, *Summa,* I, n. 194; Beste, *Introductio in Codicem,* p. 138; De Meester, *op. cit.,* I, n. 319; S. R. R., *Bononien., Iurisdictionis parochialis,* 21 iul. 1911, *coram R. P. D. Michaele Lega, Decano—AAS,* III (1911), 456 ff.

grants to the local ordinary the right to reserve their baptism to himself, in order that it may be performed with greater honor and dignity. With reference to baptism an adult is one who has attained the use of reason.[17] When such a one is to be solemnly baptized, the Code requires that the baptism be referred to the local ordinary, if this can be done conveniently, so that he, if he so desires, may administer the sacrament either personally or through his delegate.[18] It is implied in the law that the local ordinary may freely forego the use of this right and relieve the pastors of the obligation of reporting such baptisms to him.

Another possible restriction upon the pastor's exclusive right to baptize his own subjects would be the cumulative right which another pastor might have to baptize these same subjects. Before the promulgation of the Code, exclusive as well as cumulative rights could be acquired by parishes through law or custom. The Code unconditionally abrogated all exclusive rights which might have survived to that time, but cumulative rights already acquired were still recognized under the new law.[19] Hence, wherever a legitimate cumulative right existed in 1918, that right could still continue to be exercised.[20] But the attitude of the Holy See to cumulative rights is by no means one of approval, as is manifest in the response of the Commission for the Interpretation of the Code, on November 12, 1922, which declared that in the future cumulative rights could no longer be acquired by custom.[21]

In many parts of this country there exists a custom whereby converts are baptized by the priest who supervised their instruction rather than by their proper pastor. In most cases, it is true, the baptism is administered conditionally and perhaps privately as well, inasmuch as the local ordinary is empowered to permit the use of the private form in the case of heretics who as adults are baptized conditionally.[22] Such a baptism would not constitute a

---

[17] Canon 745, §2, 2º.

[18] Canon 744.

[19] Canon 774, §1.

[20] Vermeersch-Creusen, *Epitome,* II, n. 53.

[21] *AAS,* XIV (1922), 662.

[22] Canon 759, §2; cf. Prümmer, *Manuale Theologiae Moralis* (3 vols., 3. ed., Friburgi Brisgoviae, 1923), III, n. 120.

reserved parochial function. But when it is a question of solemn baptism, this practice is contrary to the prescript of the common law, and can hardly be justified unless the local ordinary, by virtue of the power which he derives from canon 738, §1, has expressly decreed that the priest who supervised the instruction may also perform the baptism.[23]

In fact, there are several reasons why this practice should be permitted and even legalized. Granted that the pastor is the lawful minister, it must also be recognized that the priest who instructs the convert has some interest in perfecting the work which he has begun. Moreover, the convert's entrance into the Church is rendered unnecessarily stiff and embarrassing when he is compelled to request his baptism at the hands of one who, though technically his proper pastor, may nevertheless be a strange and awesome personage in the eyes of the catechumen. It is the opinion of the writer that such a statute would be desirable, and would moreover serve to clarify the existing confusion in the baptism of converts.[24] Precautions should be taken, however, that the record of baptism be transmitted to the proper pastor for insertion in the parish register.[25]

Section 2. THE BAPTISM OF THOSE WHO DO NOT POSSESS A DOMICILE OR A QUASI-DOMICILE WITHIN THE PARISH

The pastor's right to administer solemn baptism to his parishioners is in no whit diminished by the latter's temporary withdrawal from the parish. According to law, the traveller must return to his own parish for the licit reception of solemn baptism, if such a journey can be undertaken conveniently and without delay.[26]

The traveller is not obliged to return to his proper pastor, however, unless both of the conditions mentioned in canon 738, §2,

[23] "Minister ordinarius baptismi est sacerdos; sed eius collatio reservatur parocho vel alii sacerdoti de eiusdem parochi *vel Ordinarii loci* licentia. . . ."

[24] Cf., for example, *Synodus Dioecesana Fargensis Prima* (Milwaukee: Bruce, 1941), Statutum 213, n. 4.

[25] Canon 778.

[26] Canon 738, §2; "De baptismo in paroecia aliena"—*Jus Pontificium,* I-II (1921-1922), 109.

are present simultaneously. If either one of them is lacking, then the absent subject may licitly receive solemn baptism from any pastor, provided that it be administered within the latter's territory.[27] It is impossible to formulate a general norm whereby the existence of these two factors could be determined: the circumstances in each case must be weighed and examined.[28] Less inconvenience would be required, for example, for the baptism of an infant outside his proper parish than would be necessary for the baptism of an adult in similar circumstances. But even in the case of the infant inconvenience must be present in some degree, before the local pastor could licitly presume to administer solemn baptism. Vermeersch-Creusen maintain that a centenary custom permitting a pastor to baptize indiscriminately any and all infants born in his parish could be tolerated by the local ordinary.[29] This opinion reveals scant respect for a venerable parochial right, and contradicts the letter as well as the spirit of canons 5, 462, §1, and 738.[30] According to canon 5, a centenary or immemorial custom contrary to the new law may be tolerated only when, in view of particular circumstances, the ordinary judges that it cannot prudently be suppressed.

In seeking to determine what extent of delay must be involved before the obligation of returning to one's proper parish ceases, one can hardly set any hard and fast rule. Waldron states that authors interpret the phrase "*sine mora*" of canon 738, §2, as being identical in meaning with the word "*quamprimum*" of canon 770.[31] It must be remembered, however, that canon 770 uses this term only with reference to the baptism of infants: it can not therefore be extended to cover the baptism of adults as well.

---

27 Cf. Waldron, *The Minister of Baptism*, p. 108.

28 Cf. "Right to Baptize Solemnly Children Born in Hospitals"—*The American Ecclesiastical Review* (Vols. I-XXXII, Philadelphia, 1895–1905; from 1905: *The Ecclesiastical Review*, Vols. XXXIII-CIX, Philadelphia, 1905–1943; from 1944: *The American Ecclesiastical Review*, Washington, D. C., Vol. CX, 1944—), LXXX (1929), 512–514 (henceforth cited *ER* and *AER* respectively).

29 *Epitome*, II, n. 23.

30 Cf. "Baptism outside of Proper Parish"—*ER*, LXXXVII (1932), 306–307.

31 *The Minister of Baptism*, p. 109.

With consideration given to the baptism of infants, the term "*quamprimum*" is commonly interpreted as signifying a period of from three to eight days.[32] Any delay, therefore, protracted beyond eight days would entitle the parents to bring the child to the local parish church for baptism. Adults too are bound to receive baptism as soon as it is morally possible, but since the principal effect of the sacrament can be attained by desire, the obligation to receive the sacrament is not as urgent as in the case of infants. It seems therefore that the delay of at least a month would be required before the right of the proper pastor can be said to be extinguished.[33]

Cappello states that the judgment concerning the unavoidability of the delay or the gravity of the inconvenience rests solely with the subject for baptism, or with his parents or guardian.[34] It must be understood, however, that the priest who is petitioned to administer solemn baptism to one who is not his subject is not freed of all responsibility by that very fact. He too is bound to make at least a cursory investigation into the circumstances before he can lawfully ratify the decision of the one petitioning, for unless some extenuating factor is present (and aside from the possibility of a canonically authorized permission), any priest who presumes to confer solemn baptism on anyone not a subject by domicile or quasi-domicile acts unlawfully. Such a practice was strongly condemned by the II Plenary Council of Baltimore (1866) as a very serious abuse.[35]

It is to be noted, finally, that when the baptism is performed by the local pastor because of the inconvenience or the delay that would be otherwise entailed, there devolves upon him the duty of

---

[32] S. C. de Prop. Fide, litt. (ad Vic. Coreae), 11 sept. 1841—*Fontes,* n. 4795; S. C. C., 31 dec. 1909—*Fontes,* n. 2065, p. 28, n. 118; Cappello, *Tractatus Canonico-Moralis de Sacramentis* (3 vols. in 6, Vol. I, 4. ed., Romae: Marietti, 1945), I, n. 141 (henceforth cited De Sacramentis); Merkelbach, *Summa Theologiae Moralis,* III, n. 148.

[33] Lehmkuhl, *Theologia Moralis* (2 vols., 9. ed., Friburgi Brisgoviae: Herder, 1898), II, n. 75; Merkelbach, *op. cit.,* III, n. 143.

[34] *Summa,* II, n. 508.

[35] *Concilii Plenarii Baltimorensis Secundi Acta et Decreta* (2. ed., Baltimore, 1880), n. 227 (hereafter cited *Acta et Decreta*).

recording the baptism in his parish register.[36] A written report of the baptism must then be sent as soon as possible to the proper pastor; the report should contain an accurate account of all the details required by law (canon 777) for making out the baptismal record.[37]

In the case of those who have no domicile or quasi-domicile, or who at most have only a diocesan domicile or quasi-domicile, the proper minister for the administration of solemn baptism is the pastor of the parish where they are actually living at the time the baptism is to be conferred.[38] His right to administer the sacrament in their behalf is equally as strong as it is in regard to those who are his subjects by virtue of domicile or quasi-domicile within the parish. He is their proper pastor as long as they continue to reside within his territory, and no other priest may presume to administer solemn baptism to such persons without violating his right.[39]

Article 2. *Holy Eucharist and Extreme Unction*

Section 1. THE SOLEMN FIRST COMMUNION OF CHILDREN

While not expressly listed in the common law as a reserved parochial function, nevertheless in some localities the administration of the solemn first Communion of children is an acknowledged parochial prerogative.[40] The practice of having general or solemn first Communions in the parish was recommended in the decree "*Quam singulare.*"[41] But whether the solemn Communion can

[36] S. C. C., 31 ian. 1927—Bouscaren, *The Canon Law Digest* (2 vols., Milwaukee: Bruce, 1934, 1943), II, 184.

[37] Cf. the Instruction of the S. C. of the Sacraments, June 29, 1941, in which under 11, d, it is stated that the baptism be recorded also in the register of the parish of origin—*AAS*, XXXIII (1941), p. 306; Bouscaren, *The Canon Law Digest*, II, 263.

[38] Canon 94, §2 and §3.

[39] Cf. Merkelbach, *Summa Theologiae Moralis*, III, n. 137; Noldin-Schmitt, *Summa Theologiae Moralis* (26. ed., 3 vols., Ratisbonae: Pustet, 1940), III, n. 64; Prümmer, *Manuale Theologiae Moralis*, III, n. 120.

[40] Vermeersch-Creusen (*Epitome*, I, n. 548) seem to point to the IV Provincial Council of Malines (1920) as having reserved this function to pastors.

[41] S. C. de Sacramentis, 8 aug. 1910, ad 5—*Fontes*, n. 2103.

be constituted a reserved parochial function by particular law is not certain. Vermeersch-Creusen maintain that such reservation is within the competence of a plenary or a provincial council, or also of a diocesan synod.[42] Cappello, on the other hand, holds that such a particular law would be derogatory of the law of the Code, in which no distinction is made between the private first Communion and the solemn first Communion.[43]

In view of the comparatively recent Instruction of the Sacred Congregation of the Sacraments on daily Communion and the precautions to be taken against possible and likely abuses, the practice of having general or solemn Communions can no longer be regarded as commendable.[44] In the mind of the Holy See the reception of Holy Communion in a body, especially in the case of young children, is fraught with the danger of abuse.[45] Since therefore the practice itself is no longer approved, it is the opinion of the writer that any discussion of its status as a reserved function would be unprofitable.

Section 2. HOLY COMMUNION FOR THE SICK

It is prescribed in the Roman Ritual that, when the Blessed Sacrament is carried to the sick, it be done so publicly and with solemnity.[46] The priest, vested in surplice, stole and cope, and proceeding under a canopy or umbrella, is to be accompanied by acolytes and a number of parishioners carrying a tinkling bell and lighted candles.[47] When performed in this manner, the carrying of the Blessed Sacrament is a function reserved exclusively to pastors, and may not be undertaken by other priests, except in a

---

[42] *Epitome,* I, n. 548.

[43] *Summa,* II, n. 520, p. 69.

[44] S. C. de Sacramentis, 8 dec. 1938—Bouscaren, *The Canon Law Digest,* II, 208.

[45] "In communities of boys and girls there should never be an announcement of a general Communion with special solemnity, and even outside communities, the very name "general Communion" should either not be used at all or its meaning should be carefully explained . . ."—*loc. cit.*

[46] "Deferri autem debet hoc sanctum Sacramentum ab ecclesia ad privatas aegrotantium domos decenti habitu. . . . publice atque honorifice. . . ."—Tit. IV, c. 4, *de communione infirmorum,* n. 6.

[47] *Ibid.,* nn. 10–12.

case of necessity or with the permission, at least presumed, of the pastor or the local ordinary.[48]

The Blessed Sacrament is said to be carried to the sick privately when the priest who carries It is dressed in street clothes and when all external solemnity is omitted, or when it is carried with all solemnity but only within the very house where the Blessed Sacrament is reserved, for example, in a convent or in a hospital.[49] With the possible exception of Spain and South America, the private mode of procedure is now the common practice, especially in the large cities including even Rome itself.[50]

The Code directs that Holy Communion be carried to the sick publicly, unless a just and reasonable cause is present to render such a mode inadvisable.[51] On December 16, 1927, the Sacred Congregation of the Sacraments was asked "whether the judge of the just and reasonable cause which, according to canon 847, is required in order that Holy Communion may be brought privately to the sick is the priest who is administering the Sacrament, or only the ordinary of the place." The Sacred Congregation replied in the negative to the first part, and in the affirmative to the second, thereby leaving the judgment exclusively in the hands of the local ordinary.[52] Despite this response of the Sacred Congregation, Cappello asserts that the judgment concerning the weight and reasonableness of the cause pertains not only to the ordinary or

---

[48] Canons 462, 2°, and 848, §2.

[49] Cappello, *Summa*, II, n. 509. For instructions on the mode of carrying Holy Communion to the sick privately, the Sacred Congregation of the Sacraments (23 dec. 1912—*Fontes*, n. 2107) made reference to §23 of the Encyclical *"Inter omnigenas"* of Benedict XIV (2 febr. 1744—*Fontes*, n. 339), which in turn is based on the regulations prescribed by the Council of Albano (1703)—Mansi, XXV, 1398-1399.

[50] Adnotationes ad S. C. C., *Romana et Aliarum*, 5 ian. 1928—*AAS*, XX (1928), 82; Bouscaren, *The Canon Law Digest*, I, 405.

[51] Canon 847. This has been the constant attitude of the Holy See: S. R. C., *Gandaven.*, 16 dec. 1826—*DA*, n. 2650; *Bisinianen.*, 23 maii 1846—*DA*, n. 2908; *Molinen.*, 12 sept. 1857, ad 19—*DA*, n. 3059; *Vicariatus Apostolici de Dania*, 10 febr. 1871, ad 1—*DA*, n. 3234; *Mantuana*, 6 febr. 1875—*DA*, n. 3337; *Templen.*, 12 ian. 1878, ad 7—*DA*, n. 3438; S. C. de Sacramentis, *Romana et Aliarum*, 23 dec. 1912—*Fontes*, n. 2107; S. C. Prop. Fide, 11 sept. 1779, n. 3—*Fontes*, n. 4581.

[52] *AAS*, XX (1928), 81; Bouscaren, *The Canon Law Digest*, I, 404.

to the pastor, but even to the confessor or to any other priest capable of carrying the Blessed Sacrament to the sick.[53] Cappello insists that the Sacred Congregation cannot take away the faculty which is extended to the latter by canon 849, §1, nor can it furnish an authentic interpretation of the canon, since this power pertains exclusively to the Pontifical Commission for the Interpretation of the Code.[54] Granted that the Sacred Congregation cannot provide an authentic interpretation, it is still difficult to understand how the instruction in question would suppress any faculty contained in Canon 848, §1.

Once the decision has been made by the local ordinary that a just and reasonable cause exists, either in all or in a part of his territory, any priest needs only the permission, at least presumed, of the rector or chaplain responsible for the custody of the Blessed Sacrament.[55] With this exception, the permission of the pastor is in no way necessary, even though the communicant be his parishioner. Beste notes that in this country it is the universal practice to carry Holy Communion privately to the sick, and that in consequence no pastor can reasonably maintain that his right is thereby violated.[56] In the II Plenary Council of Baltimore (1866) the bishops of this country regretfully sanctioned the practice of carrying the Blessed Sacrament privately to the sick.[57]

Section 3. HOLY VIATICUM AND EXTREME UNCTION

Although any priest by virtue of his sacred orders may validly administer Holy Viaticum and extreme unction, the law prescribes that the administration of the "last sacraments" be reserved to

---

[53] *Summa,* II, n. 509; cf. also Wernz-Vidal, *Ius Canonicum,* Tomus IV, vol. 1 (1934), n. 105, nota 248; Regatillo, *Ius Sacramentarium* (2 vols., Sal Terrae: Santander, 1945–1946), I, n. 311.

[54] Cf. Motu proprio, *"Cum Iuris Canonici,"* 15 sept. 1917—*AAS,* IX (1917), pars II, appendix II; this motu proprio may be consulted more conveniently among the preliminary documents listed in any copy of the Code of Canon Law.

[55] Canon 849, §1; Vermeersch-Creusen, *Epitome,* II, n. 114.

[56] *Introductio in Codicem,* p. 494.

[57] "Dolendum sane est rerum adjuncta, quae apud nos obtinent, impedire quominus ea cum pompa, quam vult Ecclesia, ad infirmos deferatur Sanctissimum Sacramentum."—*Acta et Decreta,* n. 264.

the exclusive competence of that pastor within whose territory the dying person is actually residing.[58] No other priest may licitly take upon himself the exercise of these functions unless he has the permission, at least presumed, of the local pastor or of the local ordinary, or in some case of necessity.[59] Unlike solemn baptism, the administration of the last sacraments calls for the local pastor rather than one's proper pastor. Concerning the right of the proper pastor the law is silent. Coronata is of the opinion that the proper pastor could licitly anoint a parishioner outside his own territory, thereby implying that the proper pastor would have an equal right with the local pastor to administer the last sacraments, if the circumstances of inconvenience and delay did not intervene.[60]

A distinction is to be made between Holy Viaticum strictly so-called and Holy Viaticum in its broader connotation. The former is the Communion prescribed by divine as well as ecclesiastical law when one falls into serious danger of death.[61] In its broader meaning Holy Viaticum signifies the Communion which one receives out of devotion while still seriously ill.[62] As a reserved parochial function, Holy Viaticum must be understood in the strict sense, for according to canon 19, laws which restrict the free exercise of anyone's rights are to receive a strict interpretation.[63] Extreme unction, on the other hand, may be administered but once, regardless of how long the same danger of death continues, and it is this single administration that is reserved to the local pastor.[64]

---

[58] Canons 850 and 938, §2.

[59] Canons 848, §2, and 938, §2; cf. Jorio, *La Communione agl' Infermi* (Roma: Pustet, 1931), pp. 55–60; Kilker, *Extreme Unction,* The Catholic University of America Canon Law Studies, n. 32 (Washington, D. C.: The Catholic University of America, 1926), pp. 92–101.

[60] *Tractatus Canonicus de Sacramentis* (3 vols., Romae: Marietti, 1943–1946), I, n. 548 (hereafter cited *De Sacramentis*).

[61] Canon 864, §1.

[62] Claeys Boúúaert-Simenon, *Manuale Juris Canonici,* II, n. 106; Vermeersch-Creusen, *Epitome,* II, n. 114; Regatillo, *Ius Sacramentarium,* I, n. 313.

[63] Cf. Van Hove, *Commentarium Lovaniense,* Vol. I, Tomus II, *De Legibus Ecclesiasticis* (Mechliniae: Dessain, 1930), n. 304.

[64] Canon 940, §2.

The law allows several exceptions to this parochial right. The first exception concerns the administration of the last sacraments to the bishop, and provides that this be performed by the ranking dignitary of the cathedral chapter.[65] The members of a clerical religious community, whether exempt or non-exempt, are also freed by the law from submitting to any observance of this parochial right. This includes the professed religious, the novices and any other persons residing with the community day and night as servants, students, patients or guests. The right to administer the last sacraments to them belongs to the superior of the clerical religious community.[66]

Again, in a religious community of women with solemn vows, it pertains to the ordinary confessor, rather than to the local pastor, to confer the last rites on the nuns and whatever domestics may reside in the convent day and night.[67] In the case of a lay religious society, if the bishop has appointed a chaplain to care for the spiritual needs of the community, this right belongs to the chaplain rather than to the local pastor.[68] Although not explicitly excepted in either canon 850 or 938, §2, all persons residing in a seminary must also be regarded as exempt from the parochial jurisdiction, and will receive the last sacraments from the rector of the seminary.[69] In all other cases the local pastor is the ordinary minister.

Strangely enough, the law does not make any explicit provision for the administration of the last sacraments to the pastor himself. Canon 447, §3, however, points very definitely to the dean as having a responsibility for the pastors in his deanery. It is for him "*operam dare ne* [*parochus sui districtus*] *spiritualibus . . . auxiliis . . . careat.*" It is for the dean, then, to invoke such measures whereby this obligation of administering the last sacraments to the pastors in his jurisdiction can be met either in person or through someone properly designated by him.[70]

---

[65] Canon 397, §3; for the rules of precedence, cf. canon 408.

[66] Canon 514, §1: Kilker, *Extreme Unction*, pp. 93–96.

[67] Canon 514, §2.

[68] Canon 514, §3.

[69] Canon 1368.

[70] Cf. De Meester, *Compendium Juris Canonici*, II, n. 827.

Article 3. *Matrimony and Holy Orders*

Section 1. PUBLICATION OF THE BANNS OF MARRIAGE AND PUBLIC ANNOUNCEMENT OF SACRED ORDINATION

The publication of the banns of marriage and the public announcement of sacred ordination are unique among the reserved parochial functions in that they involve purely administrative acts which have no connection with the power of orders or of jurisdiction.[71] The chief purpose of these functions is to bring to light any existing impediments to the forthcoming marriage or ordination. Although this duty has been incumbent upon pastors since the Council of Trent, it was not officially recognized as a reserved parochial function until the promulgation of the Code, and—another unique characteristic—has never in itself been the object of strife and dispute as have the other parochial prerogatives. For the sake of clarity, then, this composite function will be treated first with regard to marriage, and then as it concerns sacred ordination.

A. *Publication of the Banns of Marriage*

The Code prescribes that the banns of marriage be publicly announced by the proper pastor.[72] The importance of this function as a parochial right is not immediately evident in this country, where it is not customary to receive a stole fee for its performance. By the proper pastor is meant the pastor of that parish in which one has a domicile or quasi-domicile, or, lacking both of these, where one is actually residing.[73] As the writer has previously noted, a person can possess more than one domicile as well as more than one quasi-domicile simultaneously. The pastors of all these places will therefore be proper pastors and competent to announce the banns. Since minors share in the domicile of their parents or guardians, the banns for their marriage will be published in the parish where the parental domicile is situated, even though the minor no longer resides there.[74]

---

[71] Canon 462, 4°.

[72] Canon 1023, §1; cf. also *Rituale Romanum,* tit. 7, c. 1, *de sacramento matrimonii,* n. 6.

[73] Canon 94, §§1–3; Coronata, *De Sacramentis,* III, n. 89.

[74] Canon 93, §1; Roberts, *The Banns of Marriage,* p. 72.

According to the law, all the proper pastors, as many as they may be, have the right as well as the duty to proclaim the banns of marriage for their subjects.[75] Indeed, the publication of the banns may be described as a cumulatively reserved function, since perhaps in the majority of instances at least two pastors, namely the pastor of the bride and the pastor of the groom, will be competent to perform this function.

The right to assist validly and licitly at marriages belongs, besides to the proper pastors as determined in canon 94, also to the pastor of the place where either of the parties has completed a month's residence.[76] Some authors insist that he, too, has the right and the corresponding duty to proclaim the banns.[77] It is the more probable opinion, however, that the pastor of the month's residence is not under any obligation to publish the banns, since he is not a "*parochus proprius*" in the strict sense.[78] He is similar to a proper pastor only as regards his power to assist at marriages, and for this reason may be broadly styled a "proper" pastor, but except for the power to assist at marriages all similarity to the proper pastor ceases.[79] Since, therefore, the pastor of the

[75] Canons 462, 4º, and 1023, §1.

[76] Canon 1097, §1, 2º.

[77] Blat, *Commentarium Textus Codicis Iuris Canonici* (5 vols. in 7, Vol. III, pars I, *De Sacramentis,* 2. ed., Romae: Ex Typographia Pontificia in Instituto Pii IX, 1924), III, pars I, n. 414; Fanfani, *De Iure Parochorum* (Romae: Marietti, 1924), p. 281; Rossi, *De Matrimonii Celebratione iuxta Codicem Iuris Canonici* (Romae: Pustet, 1924), n. 13, nota 47.

[78] Cappello, *Tractatus Canonico-Moralis de Sacramentis* (3 vols. in 6, Vol. III, partes I et II, *De Matrimonio,* 4. ed., Romae: Marietti, 1939), III, pars I, n. 164, p. 207 (henceforth cited *De Matrimonio*); DeSmet, *Tractatus Theologico-canonicus de Sponsalibus et Matrimonio* (4. ed., Brugis: Car. Beyaert, 1927), n. 44, nota 3; Vlaming, *Praelectiones Iuris Matrimonii* (3. ed., 2 vols., Bussum in Hollandia: Sumptibus Societatis Editricis Anonymae, 1919, 1921), I, n. 152; De Becker, *De Matrimonio Praelectiones Canonicae* (ed. nova, Lovanii: Fr. Ceuterick, 1931), p. 154.

[79] "Nullibi canon 1097 vocat *proprium* parochum menstruae commorationis. . . . Attamen, brevitatis causa et latiore quodam sensu, ideo *proprium* nuncupamus parochum menstruae commorationis quia *jure proprio* matrinonio adsistit."—Payen, *De Matrimonio in Missionibus ac potissimum in Sinis Tractatus Practicus et Casus* (2. ed., 3 vols., Zi-ka-wei: In Typographia T'ou-se-we, 1935–1936), II, n. 1689, nota 1 (henceforth cited *De Matrimonio*).

month's residence is not a proper pastor in the strict sense, neither has he a strict right to publish the banns, nor has his local ordinary the corresponding right to dispense from their publication.[80]

B. *Public Announcement of Sacred Ordination*

With the exception of religious who have perpetual vows, whether simple or solemn, the names of candidates for each of the sacred orders are to be publicly announced in their respective parish churches.[81] Exception is made for religious who have perpetual vows, since as a consequence of their perpetual profession they lost their affiliation with their erstwhile proper diocese.[82] Another reason "*ex convenientia*" for this exception may be adduced from the fact that as religious they will not be ordained primarily for the service of the diocese, and hence their ordination need not be brought to the attention of the faithful.

Although canon 998, §1, uses the singular form (*in paroeciali cuiusque candidati ecclesia*), the law must be understood as requiring the publication of the name of the candidate in all those parishes where he may have a domicile or quasi-domicile.[83] If in his prudent judgment the proper ordinary considers that the publication when made only in the parish church will prove insufficient, he may order that the name of the candidate be proclaimed in other churches also.[84] If the other churches have their own pastor or rector, the proper pastor cannot insist that this function be reserved to himself.

Unlike the banns of marriage, only one publication is required. According to the law, the public announcement of the ordination is to be made before the reception of each of the major orders, unless the interval of time between one ordination and the next

---

[80] Canon 1028, §1; Roberts, *The Banns of Marriage,* p. 102; Gasparri, *Tractatus Canonicus De Matrimonio* (2 vols., editio nova, Romae: Typis Polyglottis Vaticanis, 1932), I, n. 158.

[81] Canon 998, §1.

[82] Canon 585; cf. Cappello, *Tractatus Canonico-Moralis de Sacramentis* (3 vols. in 6, Vol. II, pars III, *De Sacra Ordinatione,* Romae: Marietti, 1935), II, pars III, n. 546 (hereafter cited *De Sacra Ordinatione*).

[83] Cappello, *ibid.,* n. 547.

[84] Canon 998, §1; A. Villien, "L'Ordination"—*Le Canoniste Contemporain* (45 vols., Paris, 1878-1926), XLV (1922), 393.

is very brief, not more than one or two weeks.[85] In many localities there has arisen the usage of making any public announcement regarding ordinations a single time only, that is, before the reception of priesthood, letting this single publication suffice for all three major orders. In view of the explicit prescription of the law that the public announcement be made before each sacred ordination, such a usage contravenes the law of the Code and can scarcely be tolerated unless peculiar circumstances in the locality so require.[86] If circumstances warrant the omission of the public announcement before the reception of the sub-diaconal or diaconal orders, then it is within the province of the local ordinary readily to grant a dispensation from the law which requires that the announcement be made, for canon 998, §1, empowers the local ordinary to dispense from the law in the presence of any just cause.

Section 2. Assistance at Marriages

Coming now to the consideration of the most strongly entrenched of all parochial functions,[87] one finds that the assistance at marriages is so reserved to pastors as to affect the very validity of the sacrament. As in the case of Holy Viaticum and extreme unction, the reservation is made on a territorial rather than on a personal basis. Adhering closely to the discipline enacted in the decree "*Ne temere*" of 1907, the Code has prescribed that only those marriages are valid which are celebrated in the presence of the local ordinary, of the local pastor, or of a priest delegated by either of them, and in the presence also of at least two witnesses.[88] But, although the element of territoriality underlies the consideration of the marriage contract's validity, there is further required for the lawful contracting of the marriage that it be celebrated before the proper pastor. The local pastor has no right to officiate at a marriage within his territory, unless at least one of the parties has a domicile, a quasi-domicile, a month's residence, or, if he be without any settled abode (*vagus*), an

[85] Coronata, *Institutiones Iuris Canonici,* II, n. 187; Many, *De Sacra Ordinatione* (Parisiis, 1905), n. 118, p. 304.

[86] Cappello, *De Sacra Ordinatione,* n. 547.

[87] Canon 462, 4o.

[88] Canon 1094.

actual residence within the parish. If the element of residence within the parish be lacking, the permission of the pastor of the residence must be obtained, unless it is a case of urgent necessity that will brook no delay, or unless the parties have no stable dwelling place whatsoever.[89]

Thus the determination of the proper pastor for the celebration of marriage deviates slightly from the general norm expressed in canon 94, §1,[90] in that a month's residence within a parish is sufficient to constitute that juridic relationship whereby a person becomes a subject of one pastor (at least as regards the celebration of marriage) to the exclusion of all others. Unlike domicile and quasi-domicile, which require a residence in the strict sense of a settled sojourn, the month's residence will effectively serve its purpose when it has been accomplished after the fashion of a traveller's, a guest's, or a transient laborer's sojourn in any given locality.[91] The month's residence must be a fact, that is, not simply a matter that was only intended without having reached its actual execution. The month is to be computed according to the calendar, but the first day is not counted unless the beginning of residence coincided with the very beginning of that day.[92] Furthermore, the month's stay must immediately precede the marriage; any notable interruption between the fulfillment of the month's residence and the celebration of the marriage would nullify the juridical effects of the former.[93] It may be noted, finally, that

---

[89] Canon 1097, §1, 2º and 3º; *Rituale Romanum,* tit. 7, c. 1, *de sacramento matrimonii,* n. 5.

[90] " Sive per domicilium sive per quasi-domicilium suum quisque parochum et Ordinarium sortitur."

[91] Cf. Coronata, *De Sacramentis,* III, n. 555.

[92] The writer follows the opinion of Van Hove, who, in his work *Commentarium Lovaniense,* Vol. I, Tomus III *De Temporis Supputatione* (Mechliniae: Dessain, 1933), n. 305, holds that the starting point in the acquisition of the month's residence is to be regarded as a *terminus a quo* which is implicitly fixed in law—canon 34, §3, 1º–3º.

[93] S. C. de Sacramentis, *Liceitas Matrimonii,* 28 ian. 1916—*AAS,* VIII (1916), 64–66, or *Fontes,* n. 2113, in which the Sacred Congregation decided that an absence of three weeks between the completion of the month's residence and the celebration of the marriage rendered the former ineffective as a juridical basis for the local pastor's lawful assistance at the marriage.

the month's residence is in no way affected by the element of one's religious affiliation: even though a convert may have completed his month's residence before baptism, such residence could still afford a legitimate title for the licit celebration of matrimony in the locality where the month's residence was completed.[94]

Since the proper pastor of the bride and the proper pastor of the groom fundamentally enjoy equal competence for lawfully assisting at the marriage of these persons within the limits of their respective parishes, it has been prescribed as a general norm that the right of the pastor of the bride be given preference.[95] Therefore the strict parochial right to assist at marriages should be understood as belonging only to the pastor of the bride. This norm seems to be more of a directive than of a preceptive nature inasmuch as its observance can be foregone for any reasonable cause.[96] If, however, the bride should have more than one domicile, or both a domicile and a quasi-domicile, or if, while possessing any or all of these, she also have completed a month's residence elsewhere, then more than one pastor would simultaneously have a right to assist at the marriage. It is not indicated in the Code whose right should prevail in such a case. Lacking a particular law to the contrary, a freedom of choice is accorded to the contracting parties.[97] The statement of Petrovits that the pastor of the place where the bride just completed a month's residence has the least claim to witness the marriage seems to lack all legal foundation.[98]

Having outlined the salient features of the legislation governing

---

[94] *Loc. cit.*

[95] Canon 1097, §2; cf. Piontek, "Equitable Practices under Canon 1097, §2—*The Jurist,* III (1943), 456–474, for a practical study of the application of equity to this canon.

[96] Concerning the reasonable cause and its interpretation, cf. Clifford, "The Interpretation of Canon 1097"—*ER,* CVIII (1943), 122–125; Woywod, "Rules for the Licit Assistance at Marriage"—*The Homiletic and Pastoral Review* (New York, 1900—), XXIV (1924), 1056.

[97] Cf. Vlaming, *Praelectiones Iuris Matrimonii,* II, n. 582.

[98] *New Church Law on Matrimony,* The Catholic University of America Canon Law Studies, n. 6 (Washington, D. C.: The Catholic University of America, 1919), n. 489. Cf. Carberry, *The Juridical Form of Marriage,* The Catholic University of America Canon Law Studies, n. 84 (Washington, D. C.: The Catholic University of America, 1934), p. 111.

the valid and licit assistance at marriage, the writer now proposes to deal with certain problems which, while arising in connection with the assistance at marriages, have a direct bearing on this act as a function reserved to pastors.

The first problem which has to do with the very validity of the sacrament contemplates the possibility of more than one pastor enjoying jurisdiction in the same territory. Indeed, one of the almost essential attributes of a parish is that it be territorially exclusive. But when, because of diversity of languages, one parish is unable to care for all the inhabitants of a certain locality, the Holy See will permit the erection of one or more national parishes, the pastors of which will enjoy cumulative jurisdiction in the same territory.[99] Thus it can and at times does happen that three or four pastors of national parishes possess jurisdiction that is territorially co-extensive with that of the pastor of the English-speaking parish, even though the former in their actual exercise of jurisdiction are limited to those members of the given nationality who do not choose to attend the English-speaking parish.[100] But is their power to assist at marriages also restricted?

In virtue of canon 1095, §1, 2°, pastors of national parishes may, within the limits of their territory, *validly* assist at any and all marriages without any restriction as to the nationality of the parties.[101] Such assistance, although valid, would hardly be lawful, unless one of the parties is a member of the national parish. The fact that one of the parties, while not a member of the national parish, nonetheless has a domicile, a quasi-domicile or a month's residence within the territorial limits as postulated in canon 1097, §1, 2°, is not sufficient to render such assistance lawful. Cumulative jurisdiction is an abnormality not contemplated in canon 1097; moreover, the scope of the national pastor's jurisdiction is restricted, by the very nature of the national parish, to the faithful of the respective nationality. For these alone, whether they be

[99] Canon 216, §4. Cf. "National Parishes in America"—*ER*, LXVII (1927), 524.

[100] Cf. private declaration of the Sacred Congregation of the Council, January 15, 1938, and the letter of the Apostolic Delegate to the Bishops of the United States, February 17, 1938—Bouscaren, *Canon Law Digest*, II, 78.

[101] Cf. S. C. C., *Romana et Aliarum*, 1 febr. 1907—*ASS*, XLI (1907), 109, or *Fontes*, n. 4344.

members of his parish by domicile or quasi-domicile, or whether they have resided only a month within the limits of his jurisdiction, may the pastor of the national parish licitly as well as validly exercise his power to assist at marriages.[102]

Another difficulty is often encountered in the marriages of Catholics with non-Catholics. Does the general norm which gives the bride's pastor the preferred right to witness the marriage still hold when the bride is a non-Catholic? The authors who treat this question are sharply divided in their opinions. The weight of doctoral authority, however, stands behind the affirmative view to vindicate the right of the bride's pastor to witness the marriage even though she be a non-Catholic.[103] These authors without exception base their argument on the response of the Sacred Congregation of the Sacraments of January 28, 1916.[104]

In the animadversions of the consultors which were advanced preparatory to the decision, it was clearly stated that the monthly residence had been completed by the bride (a convert) before her baptism was nonetheless sufficient to constitute a title for the lawful assistance of the bride's pastor. From this statement the authors just mentioned draw the conclusion that the bride's pastor would have assisted lawfully, even if she had remained a non-Catholic. To this conclusion the writer takes exception as exceeding its premises, for in the case under consideration the bride was *de facto* baptized before her marriage, and the consultors were concerned only with the validity of the month's residence completed before baptism. Whether the pastor would have assisted lawfully before her baptism is still questionable.

The authors who deny the pastor's right when the bride is a

---

[102] Cf. "National pastors and assistance at marriage"—*ER*, LXXX (1929), 93.

[103] Cf. Ayrinhac-Lydon, *Marriage Legislation in the New Code of Canon Law* (new, revised ed., New York: Benziger Brothers, 1932), n. 247, p. 257; Carberry, *The Juridical Form of Marriage*, pp. 108–110; "The Pastor of the Bride Assists Lawfully at Marriage, even if she be a Non-Catholic"—*ER*, LXXVIII (1928), 523–524; "Coram Sponsae Parocho"—*ER*, LXIII (1920), 417–419; Ferry, *Stole Fees*, The Catholic University of America Canon Law Studies, n. 59 (Washington, D. C.: The Catholic University of America, 1930), p. 76.

[104] *AAS*, VIII (1916), 64–66, or *Fontes*, n. 2113.

non-Catholic base their objection precisely on the assertion that non-Catholics are not subject to any parochial jurisdiction.[105] At the most they would concede this right to the pastor only when it is known that the bride is validly baptized. If this opinion were carried logically to its ultimate conclusion, no pastor could lawfully baptize anyone, since it is only after baptism that one becomes subject to the ecclesiastical discipline. But if one makes the distinction between direct and indirect subjection, it becomes apparent that a non-Catholic can be indirectly subject to the law by virtue of his contracting with one who is directly subject.[106]

Falling back upon the general principle, "*ubi lex non distinguit, nec nos distinguere debemus,*" the writer is of the opinon that to the bride's pastor belongs the preferred right even in mixed marriages. If the law contains an explicit exception for marriages of mixed rites,[107] why were not marriages of mixed religion or of disparity of cult also explicitly excepted, if this were in the mind of the lawmaker? Surely the latter type of marriage is far more common than the former, especially in non-Catholic countries. But since the Code makes no such express exception, it must be concluded that mixed marriages are to be considered as subject to the general norm: "*in quolibet casu . . . . coram sponsae parocho celebretur.*" [108]

If this be the case, however, what must be thought of a diocesan statute which prescribes that mixed marriages be witnessed by the pastor of the Catholic party? Such a statute is not to be regarded as contrary to the common law, for the general norm of canon 1097, §2, bows to a just cause, and a mixed marriage in itself is a just cause for an extraordinary course of procedure.[109] Indeed, it is to be highly recommended that such a statute be enacted in

---

[105] Cf. Fanfani, *De Iure Parochorum,* n. 309; Payen, *De Matrimonio,* II, n. 1805; Woywod, *A Practical Commentary on the Code of Canon Law* (2 vols., ninth printing as edited by C. Smith, New York: J. Wagner, Inc., 1945), I, n. 1118; "Coram Sponsae Parocho"—*ER,* LXII (1920), 691.

[106] Cf. *supra,* p. 83.

[107] ". . . matrimonio autem cathlicorum mixti ritus . . . in ritu viri et coram eiusdem parocho sunt celebranda."—canon 1097, §2.

[108] Canon 1097, §2.

[109] *Contra,* Ayrinhac-Lydon, *Marriage Legislation in the New Code of Canon Law,* n. 247, p. 258.

order that mixed marriages may be handled more easily and uniformly, for in any event the duty of securing the dispensation would devolve upon the pastor of the Catholic party.

A pastor who presumes to witness a marriage without the permission of the proper pastor violates the right of the latter and is bound to restore the stole fee to the latter.[110] Under ordinary circumstances the pastor of the bride will be the proper pastor, and to him restitution of the stole fee is due in justice. If, however, the bride should have more than one proper pastor in view of a month's residence along with the possession of a quasi-domicile or of a domicile elsewhere, or by reason of a coincidence of all three, it is not clear in what manner disposition is to be made of the ill-gotten stole fee. Vlaming († 1935), Vidal († 1938) and Payen maintained that the stole fee should be divided equally among all the proper pastors, since all had an equal right to assist at the marriage.[111] Cappello and Payen exclude the pastor of the month's residence from sharing in the stole fee for the reason that he is not a proper pastor in the strict sense.[112] All the authors, however, are unanimous in desiring that the manner of restitution be more specifically determined by particular law.

Section 3. THE NUPTIAL BLESSING

When both contracting parties are Catholic, there is intimately joined to the marriage ceremony a special blessing, called the nuptial blessing, in which the Church, the Spouse of Christ, solemnly invokes upon the newly wedded couple, particularly the bride, the special blessing and protection of Almighty God for the fulfillment of the purpose which attaches to their conjugal life.[113]

[110] Canon 1097, §3.

[111] Vlaming, *Praelectiones Iuris Matrimonii,* II, n. 583; Wernz-Vidal, *Ius Canonicum,* Tom. V (3. ed., a P. Aguirre recognita, Romae: apud aedes Universitatis Gregorianae, 1946), n. 542, nota 58; Payen, *De Matrimonio,* II, n. 1810. Cf. also De Becker, *De Matrimonio Praelectiones Canonicae,* p. 149; Regatillo, *Ius Sacramentarium,* II, n. 540; Chelodi, *Ius Matrimoniale iuxta Codicem* (3. ed., Tridenti, 1921), n. 135.

[112] Cappello, *De Matrimonio,* II, n. 689; Payen, *De Matrimonio,* II, n. 1689, nota 1.

[113] The blessing consists of three prayers which are recited over the bride

Only when both parties are Catholic may this solemn blessing be imparted. If at the time of the marriage one or both parties were non-Catholic, the blessing can and should be given to them upon their subsequent conversion, even though by then they may have reached the twilight of their married life.[114] The blessing may not be given during the seasons of Lent and Advent, when the solemnization of marriage is prohibited.[115] Moreover, unless an apostolic indult has been obtained, the nuptial blessing may never be granted outside the Mass, whether it be the votive Mass "*pro sponso et sponsa*" or the Mass of the day.[116] Once a bride has received the blessing, she may never receive it again, even though upon her husband's death she should re-marry.[117]

Like assistance at marriage, the bestowal of the nuptial blessing is a function reserved to pastors.[118] As a parochial function, the nuptial blessing must be understood to be reserved only to that pastor who can validly and licitly assist at the marriage, namely the proper pastor.[119] In practice the minister of the nuptial blessing will be determined by the general norm which governs assistance at marriage, and which accords priority to the right of the bride's proper pastor.[120] In any event nothing prevents the proper pastor from personally assisting at the marriage though he have

---

during Mass, two being said after the *Pater Noster,* and the third after the *Benedicamus Domino* or *Ite, Missa est—Missale Romanum, Missa Votiva pro Sponso et Sponsa.* Cf. Bouscaren-Ellis, *Canon Law, A Text and Commentary,* 526–530.

[114] S. C. S. Off., 31 aug. 1881—*Fontes,* n. 1071.

[115] Canon 1108, §2. Local ordinaries can for a just cause permit the solemn blessing of marriages during the forbidden times—canon 1108, §3.

[116] Canon 1101, §1; S. R. C., *Limburgen.,* 23 iun. 1853—*Fontes,* n. 5967; *Sacrae Congregationis de Propaganda Fide,* 20 aug. 1870—*Fontes,* n. 6033; *Bergomen.,* 18 aug. 1884, ad 1—*Fontes,* n. 6158; *Romana,* 9 maii, 1893, ad IV—*Fontes,* n. 6226; *Belemen. de Para,* 12 febr. 1909—*Fontes,* n. 6372.

[117] *Rituale Romanum,* tit. 7, c. 1, *de sacramento matrimonii,* n. 18; Coronata, *Institutiones Iuris Canonici,* III, n. 576.

[118] Canon 462, 4°; Gasparri, *De Matrimonio,* II, n. 1047.

[119] Canon 1101, §2. The term "proper pastor" is here to be taken in its broad sense as including the pastor of a month's residence—canon 1097, §1, 2°.

[120] Canon 1097, §2.

authorized some other priest to offer the Mass and to impart the solemn blessing.[121]

If the nuptial blessing is to be imparted outside the Mass, an apostolic indult is required.[122] Among the quinquennial faculties which the local ordinaries of the United States enjoy there is contained the faculty which empowers them to bestow the nuptial blessing outside the Mass; the ordinary can sub-delegate to another this right to bestow the nuptial blessing outside the Mass.[123] Hence, it is evident that the bestowal of the nuptial blessing constitutes a reserved parochial function only when it is imparted during the Mass; outside the Mass a sub-delegation must be secured from the local ordinary for the imparting of the nuptial blessing.[124]

Articles 4. The Right of Pastors to Administer Confirmation in Virtue of the Apostolic Indult of September 14, 1946

A treatise on the reserved parochial functions could justly be considered incomplete if it omitted mention of the apostolic indult of September 14, 1946, wherein pastors were accorded the power to confirm the dying under certain conditions.[125] In the strict sense, however, the new faculty does not constitute a reserved parochial function, for (a) it comes by way of an apostolic indult, which by nature is only temporary and has not the permanent stability of law, and (b) it is surrounded by so many restrictions and detailed requirements that its character as a right is overshadowed by the concomitant obligations. But since the new faculty does connote an element of parochial right, it is deserving of some consideration from this aspect.

In order to provide effectively for those souls who depart this life without the opportunity of receiving the sacrament of confirmation, the Holy See has accorded to all territorial pastors the

---

[121] Cf. Coronata, *Institutiones Iuris Canonici,* III, n. 576; Cappello, *De Matrimonio,* II, n. 710.

[122] Cf. *Rituale Romanum,* Appendix I, *de matrimonio,* for the special form of the blessing when imparted outside the Mass.

[123] Cf. Bouscaren, *Canon Law Digest,* II, 37.

[124] The ordinary is empowered to sub-delegate the habitual exercise of this faculty—Canon 199, §2; cf. Ayrinhac-Lydon, *Marriage Legislation in the New Code of Canon Law,* p. 273.

[125] S. C. de Sacramentis, *Decretum—AAS,* XXXVIII (1946), 349–358.

power to administer this sacrament under certain conditions. The person to be confirmed must be in serious danger of death which is due to disease, not to accidental injury. Moreover the pastor may not use this faculty if a bishop, even a titular bishop, is available.

When the requisite conditions are present, the pastor may validly and licitly confer the sacrament on any member of the faithful within the parish limits. It makes no difference if the person is not a subject of the pastor; in fact, even those persons who reside in seminaries, hospitals or similar institutions, as well as all religious, even exempt, may validly and licitly receive confirmation at the hands of the local pastor under the given conditions.[126]

On the other hand, the power to administer confirmation in danger of death has been granted exclusively to territorial pastors and those who are made equivalent to them in the indult. Hospital chaplains, superiors of clerical religious communities and rectors of seminaries must have recourse to the local pastor if one of their subjects should fall into the danger of dying without the benefit of this sacrament. The pastor's right to adminster confirmation by virtue of the indult is most exclusive. No other priest could validly confirm within the parish limits, unless it be the pastor of a national parish, who has cumulative jurisdiction over the same territory. It is to be noted, finally, that the power to confirm in danger of death is given to pastors personally, hence it must be exercised personally and cannot be delegated.[127]

---

[126] *Ibid.*, p. 352, n. 2.

[127] *Loc. cit.*

CHAPTER V

ECCLESIASTICAL BURIAL AS A RESERVED PAROCHIAL FUNCTION

AMONG the reserved parochial functions enumerated in canon 462 may be found the right to conduct burials (" *iusta funebria persolvere* ").[1] In seeking to determine the precise signification the term " *iusta funebria* " one necessarily must recur to Title 12 of Book Three of the Code, wherein the notion of ecclesiastical burial is treated in detail, particularly in chapter 2, *de cadaveris translatione ad ecclesiam, funere ac depositione.*[2]

Strangely enough, however, among the various names which are used in Title 12 in connection with ecclesiastical sepulture, the word " *funebria* " does not occur. Even in canon 1216, which is explicitly indicated in canon 462, 5°, as containing more detailed norms for the exercise of this reserved function, the word " *funebria* " is not employed. There the predominant term is " *funus,*" which is defined in the preceding canon to be the complete funeral ritual as described in the approved liturgical books of the Catholic Church.[3] As it is presented in the Roman Ritual,[4] " *funus* " may be said to comprise five distinct and separable parts: (1) the transfer of the body to the church in which the funeral services are to take place (*levatio et associatio corporis*); (2) the recitation of the Office of the Dead; (3) the Mass of Requiem; (4) the prayers of absolution; (5) the burial.[5]

[1] Canon 462, 5°. Unless it appears otherwise from the context, the word "burial" or "burial service" will be used synonymously with the word "funeral" to signify the order of rites and ceremonies prescribed for ecclesiastical burial by the Roman Ritual, in whatever degree of totality they are customarily employed.

[2] Canons 1215 to 1238 inclusively.

[3] Canon 1215.

[4] Tit. VI.

[5] Cf. Many, *Praelectiones Canonicae de Locis Sacris* (Parisiis, 1904), n. 188; Rossi, *La " Sepultura Ecclesiastica " e L' " Ius Funerum " Nel Diritto Canonico* (Bergamo: Libreria Editrice Vescovile, 1920), pp. 65–75.

From the relation that exists between canons 462, 5°, and 1216, it is reasonable to infer that "*funebria*" has the same meaning as "*funus*" and accordingly comprises the five elements contained in the Roman Ritual. However, it must be noted that the five parts are distinct and separable, and very often the burial service is not performed in its entirety. For a just reason one or more parts of the burial service may be omitted. Therefore it is reserved to pastors to perform the "IUSTA *funebria*," i.e., the burial service in that degree of totality which is fitting and proper under the particular circumstances. In the United States, for example, "*iusta funebria*" usually does not include the recitation of the Office of the Dead.

Article 1. *The Ordinary Law Governing Ecclesiastical Burial*

Section 1. BURIAL OF THE FAITHFUL WHO DIE WITHIN THEIR PROPER PARISH

As in the time of Pope Boniface VIII (1294–1303), so today the law of ecclesiastical burial is based on the general principle that the right to conduct the burial service pertains to the priest who, during the life of the deceased, had faithfully administered to his spiritual needs, namely the proper pastor.[6] According to the ordinary law, therefore, the church to which the body ought to be transferred for the "*funus*" is the proper parish church of the deceased.[7]

As previously noted in Chapter III of this dissertation,[8] a proper parish is acquired through domicile or quasi-domicile, or, lacking both of these, by means of actual residence within the parish. According to the common law, every pastor has a legitimate right to demand that the funeral services of his parishioners be held in the parish church, and, if the parish possesses its own cemetery, that the burial take place in the parish cemetery. Prescinding from the circumstance of inconvenience, in only two

[6] C. 2, *de sepulturis*, III, 12, in VI°.

[7] Canon 1212, §1; Cocchi, *Commentarium in Codicem Iuris Canonici* (8 vols. in 5, Vol. V [Lib. III, *De Rebus;* Pars II, *De locis et temporibus sacris;* Pars III, *De cultu divino*], 4. ed., Taurinorum Augustae: Marietti, 1938), V, n. 61 (hereafter cited *Commentarium*).

[8] P. 69.

instances does the law permit an exception to this right, namely when the deceased has indicated his desire that the burial services take place elsewhere, or in the event that the deceased is to be buried in the family sepulcher which is situated in a cemetery belonging to a church other than the proper parish church.[9] The parochial right, however, enjoys the favor of the law: in any case of doubt (for example, whether the deceased elected to be buried elsewhere), the right of the proper pastor prevails.[10]

If the deceased belonged to more than one parish by reason of a plurality of domiciles, or at least through the possession of a quasi-domicile together with a domicile, then more than one pastor would be competent to officiate at the funeral services. For this reason a general rule is enacted in the law that if two or more pastors have an equal right to conduct the burial, then the favor of the law is accorded to the pastor in whose parish the person resided at the moment of death.[11]

A fairly common example of the possible application of this principle is had in the death of persons temporarily residing in a hospital, a college or a hotel. If one should have resided in such an institution for more than half a year, or if one had at least the intention of residing there for that length of time, he would have acquired a quasi-domicile by that very fact. Hence the local pastor would also be a proper pastor, and he, rather than the pastor of domicile, would be entitled to conduct the funeral in virtue of the general norm enumerated in canon 1216, §2.[12] The Code expressly treats of these special cases in canon 1222, and declares that they are to be handled according to the ordinary law governing ecclesiastical burial, while at the same time allowing for the possible existence of contrary particular laws or privileges.[13]

---

[9] These two exceptions will be considered in the succeeding section of this article.

[10] Canon 1217; Cappello, *Summa,* II, n. 722.

[11] Canon 1216, §2.

[12] S. C. C., *Melevitana,* 2 iun. 1917—*AAS,* X (1918), 328; Cocchi, *Commentarium,* V, n. 58; Capello, *Summa,* II, n. 730.

[13] Canon 1222.

Section 2. BURIAL OF THE FAITHFUL WHO DIE OUTSIDE THEIR PROPER PARISH

If death occurred in none of the proper parishes, then there prevails the right of that proper pastor whose parish is nearest to the place of death, provided that the distance is not so great that the body cannot conveniently be carried on foot to the church.[14]

That the pastor of the nearest proper *parish* has the right to bestow the burial is the common teaching of canonists; there are some, however, who interpret the canon in the sense that the nearest parish *church,* not the nearest parish, is the deciding factor.[15] It is their opinion that the word "*quae*" in the phrase "*in ecclesiam paroeciae propriae quae vicinior sit*" should be understood as relating to "*ecclesiam.*" The more common opinion seems more tenable, since it is based on a comparison with the word "*qua*" in the phrase "*in ecclesiam paroeciae in qua mors accidit,*" as well as on the general grammatical principle that a pronoun usually refers to the nearer noun.[16]

It is to be carefully noted, however, that when death has occurred beyond the confines of the proper parish, the right of the proper pastor is contingent upon the distance lying between the place of death and the parish church. If the distance is so great that the body cannot conveniently be carried on foot to the proper parish church, then the right of the proper pastor is extinguished, and the local pastor becomes competent to conduct the burial.[17] In this age of mechanical achievement, the body is usually conveyed to the church in an automotive hearse, but the outmoded

---

[14] Canon 1218, §1: "Licet mors acciderit extra propriam paroeciam, cadaver tamen in ecclesiam paroeciae propriae quae vicinior sit, ob funus transferendum est, si ad eam commode pedestri itinere asportari possit; secus in ecclesiam paroeciae in qua mors accidit." Cf. Vermeersch-Creusen, *Epitome,* II, n. 529.

[15] Cappello, *Summa,* II, n. 723, nota 2; Woywod, "The Law of the Code on Funerals,"—*The Homiletic and Pastoral Review,* XXVI (1925–1926), 612; Ayrinhac, *Administrative Legislation in the New Code of Canon Law* (New York: Longmans, Green & Co., 1930), n. 61.

[16] Cf. Coronata, *De Locis et Temporibus Sacris* (Augustae Taurinorum: Marietti, 1922), n. 167.

[17] Canon 1218, §1; Claeys Boúúaert-Simenon, *Manuale Juris Canonici,* III, n. 42.

custom of bearing the body to the church on foot is the manner prescribed by the Roman Ritual [18] and still serves as the basic norm in the determination of funeral rights.[19]

Authors generally agree that in normal circumstances a body can be carried conveniently on foot any distance within the limit of two miles.[20] Should the distance exceed this limit, it seems that the right of the proper pastor must give way in the face of the difficulty that its exercise would entail, whereupon the right of the local pastor would become operative. The distance should be computed, not as a straight line between two points, but rather according to the route along which the funeral cortege would proceed.[21]

It must be clearly understood that this rule of measurement is to be regarded only as an indicative norm which is to be further specified by particular law so as to conform to local conditions. Indeed, the Code expressly prescribes that the local ordinaries, after carefully studying local circumstances, enact more detailed regulations concerning the limits of convenience and the physical extent of the parochial prerogatives in the matter of funerals.[22] Certainly in a country like the United States, where almost exclusively the automobile is used for the conveyance of the body to the church, a general allowance could be made for an appreciably greater distance than two miles if the factor of inconvenience is to be acknowledged as militating against the transfer of the body to the proper parish church.

Even when the distance exceeds the limit fixed by particular law, a further circumstance must be considered before it can be said that the proper pastor has lost his right to conduct the burial. Relatives or friends of the deceased may be willing to meet the expenses which the greater inconvenience in conveying the body to the proper parish church would entail. Perhaps some parish

[18] Tit. 6, cap. 3, *Exsequiarum Ordo,* nn. 1, 2.

[19] Cf. Beste, *Introductio in Codicem,* 590; Vermeersch-Creusen, *Epitome,* II, n. 529.

[20] Cappello, *Summa,* II, n. 724; Coronata, *De Locis et Temporibus Sacris,* n. 168.

[21] Coronata, *loc. cit.*

[22] Canon 1218, §2; Wernz-Vidal, *Ius Canonicum,* Tomus IV, Vol. I (Romae: Apud Aedes Universitatis Gregorianae, 1934), n. 600.

sodality of which the deceased was a member may have a special fund for this purpose; it can even be imagined that the proper pastor himself would be willing to forego all or part of his stole fee in order that the body could be transferred to his parish church for the funeral. In any of these instances the proper pastor retains his right to conduct the funeral; should the local pastor take it upon himself to conduct the funeral, he would act unlawfully and would be bound in justice to restore the stole fee to the proper pastor.[23]

Article 2. *Exceptions to the Ordinary Law*

Section 1. THE RIGHT OF FREE CHOICE

Having established the general principle that the right to officiate at burial services belongs to the proper pastor, the supreme legislator then proceeds to enunciate another general principle, which seemingly runs contrary to the first: every member of the faithful, with the exception of professed religious and children below the age of puberty, has the right to select the church for his funeral and the cemetery for his burial.[24] The conflict is only apparent, however, for the right of free choice is more fundamental than the right of the proper pastor, and when the former is duly exercised, it takes precedence over the latter.

It is to be noted that the object of the free choice is twofold: (a) the choice of the church where the funeral services are to be conducted, and (b) the choice of the cemetery where the burial is to be bestowed. In countries where it is the practice to have large cemeteries for the various centers of population throughout the diocese, the possible invoking of the latter choice may not be fully appreciated, unless one realizes that according to the law of the Church each parish ought to have, if possible, its own individual cemetery.[25] Moreover, every exempt religious com-

[23] Canon 1218, §3. If the deceased belonged to several proper parishes, the relatives or friends would not be under any obligation to convey the body to the nearest proper parish, for in these circumstances none of the proper pastors has an absolute right to conduct the funeral—Coronata, *De Locis et Temporibus Sacris,* n. 169, nota 2.

[24] Canons 1223, 1224; concerning the age of puberty, cf. canon 88, §2.

[25] Canon 1208, §1.

munity enjoys the right of possessing its own cemetery, in which burial can be granted to any member of the faithful who has legitimately requested it.[26] In many countries civil ordinances and reasons of public health will not permit that this ideal be realized, wherefore the right of free choice is very often by force of circumstances restricted completely and simply to the selection of the church where the funeral services are to take place.

In order that the right of free election regarding the church of the funeral and the place of burial may prevail over the right of the proper pastor, four conditions must be verified. First, the choice must have been freely made. The supreme legislator severely warns both the secular and the religious clergy against actively inducing the faithful to select their churches for the funeral or their cemeteries for the burial; a choice made under the influence of such inducement is null.[27] Secondly, the choice must have been made by the deceased person, not by his heirs. No one may make this choice for another, unless it be a father choosing for his child who died before attaining the age of puberty.[28] Thirdly, the choice must fall upon a church which has, either by law or by privilege, the right of conducting burials.[29] Finally, the fact of the choice must be proved either by credible witnesses, by incontrovertible documents, or in some other legitimate manner.[30] Should a prudent doubt arise concerning the existence of the free choice or the presence of its essential conditions, the right of the proper pastor will prevail.[31]

In the event that a parishioner should choose a church other than his parish church for his funeral, what rights, if any, accrue to the proper pastor? If the church selected lie outside the proper parish, or if it enjoy exemption from the parochial jurisdiction, even though it be situated within the territory of the parish, the

[26] Canons 1208, §2, and 1209, §1. Cf. O'Brien, *The Exemption of Religious in Church Law* (Milwaukee: Bruce, 1942), p. 148.

[27] Canon 1227. Blat, *Commentarium Textus Codicis Iuris Canonici,* II, (*De Personis*), n. 85.

[28] Canon 1224, 1o.

[29] Canon 1225.

[30] Canon 1226, §1; S. C. C., *Dianen.,* 9 iul. 1921—*AAS,* XIII (1921), 535; *Gallipolitana,* 24 maii et 15 nov. 1930—*AAS,* XXV (1933), 157.

[31] Canon 1217.

proper pastor will have only the right to conduct the cortege to the church selected, in the manner described in the Roman Ritual.[32] If, however, the church chosen for the funeral lie within the parish limits and be not exempt, the proper pastor has the right to perform all the funeral services, including the exequies within the church, unless there exists a particular privilege to the contrary.[33] In any event, the proper pastor is entitled to receive the canonical portion of the funeral perquisite, the notion of which will be considered in the subsequent article of this chapter.

Section 2. ANCESTRAL TOMBS

The right accorded to pastors by ordinary law to conduct the burial of their parishioners allows for another exception, namely, when the deceased is to be buried in a family tomb which is situated in a cemetery belonging to another church. While preserving intact the privilege of free choice, the supreme legislator has directed that those who possess an ancestral sepulcher are to be buried there, if this can be accomplished conveniently.[34]

If the family tomb is situated within the confines of the proper parish, the rights of the proper pastor will in no way be curtailed. If, however, the family tomb is situated in a cemetery belonging to another church, it is there that the burial should take place. If the church to which the cemetery belongs has been accredited with the right of conducting funerals, the question may well arise: does the right to conduct the funeral exequies belong to the proper pastor or to the rector of the church where the burial is to take place?

Although the law prescribes that the deceased be buried in the family sepulcher, nothing is stated concerning the church in which the exequies are to take place.[35] Speculation arose whether or

[32] Canon 1230, §3; *Rituale Romanum,* Tit. VI, cap. 3 *Exsequiarum Ordo,* nn. 1, 2. In the United States this part of the burial service usually is not observed.

[33] Canon 1230, §4.

[34] Canon 1229, §1. A wife is to be buried in the family sepulcher belonging to her husband; if she had had more than one husband consecutively, her burial will take place in the family tomb of her last spouse—canon 1229, §2.

[35] "Si quis, sepulcrum maiorum in aliquo coemeterio possidens, non electa

not the Code departed from the old law, which had recognized the axiom " ubi tumulus ibi funus " as an accepted legal principle.[36] The question was addressed to the Pontifical Commission for the Interpretation of the Code, which, on January 4, 1946, replied that the possession of a family sepulcher need not be regarded also as a legitimate choice of church for the funeral services.[37]

Hence it follows that even though the burial take place in a cemetery belonging to a church other than the parish church, the proper pastor will nonetheless have the right to conduct the funeral services in the parish church, unless: (a) a contrary provision has been incorporated in the original erection of the family tomb; (b) a particular statute has decreed *" ubi tumulus, ibi funus "*; or (c) the deceased had chosen a church other than his parish church for the funeral services. This much at least is certain, that if the family tomb is situated in a public cemetery over which no individual church enjoys any special funeral rights, it pertains to the proper pastor to conduct the funeral services, provided again that there be no particular law or privilege to the contrary.

Section 3. SPECIAL LAW GOVERNING CERTAIN CLASSES OF THE FAITHFUL

Special regulations are enacted in the Code concerning the burial of certain classes of the faithful, which in effect constitute a limitation upon the funeral rights which are accorded to the proper pastor by ordinary law. Thus a canon, if he resides in a parish other that in which his benefice is located, enjoys exemption from the jurisdiction of the local pastor in the matter of ecclesiastical burial. The law prescribes that his funeral take place in the church of his benefice.[38] So also all professed male

alibi sepultura, decesserit, in eodem *sepeliendus* est, si illuc commode asportari possit,"—canon 1229, §1. (Italics inserted by the writer).

[36] S. C. C. Apuana, 12 nov. 1927 (*AAS*, XX, 144); Vermeersch, "'Ubi tumulus, ibi funus' . . . Axioma?"—*Periodica de Re Canonica et Morali utili praesertim Religiosis et Missionariis* (Bruges, 1905; ab anno 1927: *Periodica de Re Morali, Canonica, Liturgica*), XVI (1927), 57–70 (henceforth cited *Periodica*).

[37] *AAS*, XXXVIII (1946), 162.

[38] Canon 1220. Honorary canons are not included; S. C. C., 16 dec., 1939 —*AAS*, XXXII (1940), 75.

religious and male novices are to be buried from the church or oratory attached to their religious house, or, lacking this, at least from a church belonging to their order or congregation.[39] If death occurred in a place where no church of their order or congregation is conveniently at hand, the funeral is to be conducted from the local parish church. It is to be noted that novices, unlike the professed religious, still enjoy the privilege of a free choice regarding the church at which their funeral services are to be held and the place in which burial is to be bestowed. Legislation affecting their burial must be understood as being conditioned according to the presence or the absence of this optional factor.

The laws governing the burial of novices apply also to lay servants of the religious community who have a permanent residence in the religious house, provided that their death occurred in the house; if they died outside the religious house, their burial is governed by the ordinary law.[40] Postulants are not mentioned in the canon which deals with the burial of professed religious and novices. In the first decade after the enactment of the Code canonists disputed whether the special provisions enacted therein pertained to them also. The dispute was settled on July 20, 1929, when the Pontifical Commission for the Interpretation of the Code declared that postulants were not included among those subject to the special regulations of canon 1221.[41] Postulants, like those of the laity who reside in the religious house day and night either for reasons of health or education, or simply as

[39] Canon 1221, §1. Special provision is made for female religious and female novices in canon 1230, §5. If they belong to a community which is subject to the jurisdiction of the local pastor, the pastor has the right to escort the body to the parish church and there officiate at the burial services. If, however, the bishop has withdrawn the community from the jurisdiction of the pastor by assigning a chaplain to care for their spiritual needs, the funeral rights belong to the latter—cf. Response of the Pontifical Commission for the Interpretation of the Code, January 31, 1942, *AAS*, XXXIV (1942), 50.

[40] Canon 1221, §3; De Meester, *Juris Canonici et Juris Canonico-Civilis Compendium*, Tomus III, Pars I, n. 1193.

[41] *AAS*, XXI (1929), 573; cf. Creusen, *Religious Men and Women in the Code* (4. English ed. revised and edited to conform with the 5. French ed. by A. Ellis, Milwaukee: Bruce, 1940), p. 114.

boarders, are governed by the ordinary law in all that pertains to ecclesiastical burial.[42]

Article 3. *The Parochial Portion*

It is an ancient and approved custom for the family of the deceased, on the occasion of a funeral, to offer a moderate honorarium to the minister of burial, in payment for the funeral expenses and as a contribution to his temporal support. According to the ordinary law, the minister is the proper pastor, than whom there is none more deserving of receiving this funeral offering. Even when the funeral takes place in a church other than the proper parish church, equity demands that at least a portion of the funeral stipend be given to him who, during the life of the deceased, faithfully ministered to his spiritual needs.

Accordingly, the Code prescribes that whenever the funeral of a member of the faithful is not held in the proper parish church (for some reason other than the inconvenience which the transfer of the body to the proper parish church would necessitate), a share of the stipend is due to the proper pastor, provided that there be no particular statute, custom or privilege to the contrary.[43] This "canonical portion," as it is often called, is to be paid, not by the heirs, but by the rector of the church in which the funeral services took place, out of the emoluments he received on the occasion of the funeral.

Prescinding from the circumstance of inconvenience, ecclesiastical burial may legitimately take place outside the proper parish church (a) when the privilege of free choice has been exercised, and (b) when the family tomb is situated in a cemetery belonging to a church other than the proper parish church, and the right to conduct the exequies is accorded to the church where the burial is to take place. If in either of these instances the body could

[42] Canon 1222. Those who dwell in a seminary are exempt from parochial jurisdiction; the right to officiate at their burial belongs to the rector of the seminary—canon 1368.

[43] Canon 1236, §1. The rector of a seminary, the religious superior, and the chaplain of a religious community or of a hospital which has been withdrawn from parochial jurisdiction are equivalent to the proper pastor regarding the right to receive the canonical portion.

conveniently have been brought to the proper parish church (this to be determined by particular law), the canonical portion must be rendered to the proper pastor. When, however, the distance to the proper parish church is so great as to entail inconvenience in the transfer of the body to the proper parish church, the local pastor (or the rector of the church selected by the deceased, or the rector of the church where the family tomb is located) may legitimately conduct the funeral without being under any obligation to render the canonical portion to the proper pastor.[44]

If the deceased belonged to more than one proper parish, in any of which the funeral services could conveniently have taken place, the canonical portion is to be divided among the proper pastors, provided that all of them had an equal right to conduct the burial.[45] For if the parishioner died in one of the proper parishes and then is buried from the church of his choice which is not a proper parish, the canonical portion is owed in its entirety to the proper pastor of the place of death, since he had the preferred right to conduct the funeral services.[46]

It sometimes happens that the funeral exequies are not carried out until some days or weeks after the burial. If the "first solemn funeral service" is held within one month from the day of burial, the emoluments which were received on this occasion are also to be shared with the proper pastor.[47] This law holds even though some simple service was held on the day of the burial. The law does not define the precise nature of the first solemn funeral service, but it seems to postulate at least the celebration of a High Mass of Requiem.[48]

The determination of the amount of the canonical portion is left to the competence of the local ordinary. In the earlier law the canonical portion often consisted of one-fourth of all the emoluments received on the occasion of the burial, and hence it was called the "*quarta funerum.*" However, the amount need not necessarily consist of an exact one-fourth. The amount may be

[44] Coronata, *De Locis et Temporibus Sacris,* n. 248, p. 254.

[45] Canon 1236, §2.

[46] Cappello, *Summa,* n. 756; Beste, *Introductio in Codicem,* p. 602.

[47] Canon 1237, §2.

[48] S. R. C., 1 maii, 1942—*AAS,* XXXIV (1942), 205.

either a greater or a lesser one, according to the prudent judgment of the local ordinary. When the canonical portion is due to a pastor of another diocese, the amount is to be determined in accordance with the fee as fixed by diocesan law for the church from which the exequies are conducted.[49]

In some dioceses the local ordinary has seen fit to approve the accepted custom of not sending the canonical portion to the proper pastor. The acceptability of this custom is based on the theory that the losses occasioned through the observance of the custom will be offset by corresponding gains over a sufficiently lengthy period of time.

---

[49] Canon 1237, §3. Cf. Petit, *La Part Paroissiale ou Quarte Funéraire,* Les Thèses Canoniques de Laval, Thèse n. 5 (Québec: Université Laval, 1946), p. 214.

CHAPTER VI

LITURGICAL FUNCTIONS RESERVED TO PASTORS

Article 1. *Exclusive Competence in the Bestowal of Certain Blessings*

Section 1. THE NOTION OF LITURGICAL BLESSINGS

THE word "blessing" in its generic sense embraces a wide diversity of meanings, all of which have in common the idea of a spiritual or temporal good. In the sense of an action, a blessing need not be restricted to a religious signification; it may mean any form or act whereby one invokes happiness upon another. In the present article, however, the word will be considered only in the sense of an official ecclesiastical blessing.

Blessings abound in every phase of the liturgical life of the Church, yet they are but a species of that more generic source of grace called the sacramental. The Code defines the sacramental to be "a thing or an action which the Church uses, somewhat after the fashion of a sacrament, to obtain through her prayer some benefit which is usually of a spiritual nature."[1] The sacramentals are similar to the sacraments in that they are perceptible to the senses, and usually have some spiritual effect as their end; unlike the sacraments, however, they do not produce sanctifying grace in virtue of their very use and application (*ex opere operato*), nor were they instituted by Christ, but by His Church. The sacramentals derive their peculiar efficacy from the fact that they are accompanied with the official prayers of the Church, the Spouse of Christ, and as such have an inestimable value before God.[2] In general, the sacramentals are divided into three groups: exorcisms, blessed articles and blessings.

---

[1] Canon 1144; Claeys Bouúaert-Simenon, *Manuale Juris Canonici,* II, n. 348.

[2] Cf. Noldin-Schmitt, *Summa Theologiae Moralis,* III, n. 51.

As a species of the sacramentals, a blessing may be defined as a rite (in the liturgical sense of a sacred action) performed by a sacred minister in the name of the Church for the purpose of obtaining from God some suitable spiritual or temperal benefit with respect to persons or things.[3] The rite may consist of a simple sign of the cross, or in the pronunciation of a certain formula together with the sign of the cross; it may be accompanied with the sprinkling of holy water or the unction of holy oils. But whether the rite be simple or complex, it is a condition essential to the very validity of the blessing that the rite be performed according to the manner prescribed by the Church.[4]

When considered from the point of view of the effect which they produce, blessings may be divided into two general classes: constitutive blessings and invocative blessings.[5] The former, usually bestowed upon material objects, is that blessing whereby a thing (for example, a bell, baptismal water, chrism) is set apart for the divine cult and rendered permanently sacred, in such wise that henceforth it must be accorded reverent treatment and be not employed in profane service.[6] The invocative blessing on the other hand does not effect any change in the status of the person or thing blessed, but simply calls upon the divine favor, either to grant some particular good (for example, bodily health, as in the blessing of throats on St. Blaise Day), or to avert some special evil (for example, in the blessing of a fire engine), depending on the precise nature of the blessing.[7]

When considered from the point of view of the minister, blessings may be divided into reserved and non-reserved blessings. The latter may be bestowed by any priest;[8] the former, however, may be imparted only by those to whom their exercise is reserved.[9] Some blessings may be imparted only by the Pope (for example,

---

[3] Cf. *Periodica,* XVI (1927), 18*.

[4] Canon 1148, §2.

[5] S. R. C., *Veronen.,* 27 aug. 1836—*DA,* n. 2745.

[6] Canon 1150.

[7] Cf. *Periodica,* XVI (1927), 21*.

[8] Non-reserved blessings may be found in the Roman Ritual, tit. VIII, capita 1–19, and in the Appendix, under "*Benedictiones non Reservatae.*"

[9] Canon 1147, §2.

the blessing of the pallium, of the golden rose), others by bishops (for example, the blessing of abbots, of virgins, of the holy oils).[10] Some blessings are reserved to the members of a certain religious order (for example, the blessing of the stations of the cross), while other blessings have been entrusted to the exclusive competence of pastors. In the succeeding sections of this article, consideration will be devoted to this latter group of blessings.

Section 2. THE BLESSING OF HOMES ON HOLY SATURDAY

In the blessing of homes on Holy Saturday, as in all the other ecclesiastical blessings, the beauty and sanctity of the sacred liturgy is strikingly manifested. Recalling how on the first Pasch the blood of the lamb had protected the homes of the Israelites from the sword of the avenging angel, the priest in blessing a home on Holy Saturday prays God to send His holy angel to guard and defend all who dwell within it.[11] It is greatly to be regretted that in many regions, due to the scarcity of ministers or in consequence of other circumstances, this beautiful blessing has fallen into desuetude. Wherever the practice still flourishes, however, its administration remains within the competence of the pastor.[12] It is to be noted that the pastor enjoys exclusive competence over the blessing of the homes in his parish solely with reference to the solemn form which is prescribed for Holy Saturday. With this one exception, any priest may legitimately undertake privately to bless a home without infringing upon the prerogatives of the local pastor.[13]

Under the pre-Code law the question arose whether the administration of this blessing could be anticipated when, because of the size of the parish, it would be impossible to bless all the homes on Holy Saturday. The Sacred Congregation of Rites forbade the anticipatory administration of the blessing, but declared that under such circumstances the blessing could be im-

---

[10] Cf. Augustine, *Commentary*, IV, 563; Claeys Boúúaert-Simenon, *Manuale Juris Canonici*, II, n. 350.

[11] *Rituale Romanum*, tit. VIII, c. 4.

[12] Canon 462, 6o.

[13] Cf. Cappello, *Summa*, II, n. 515; Fanfani, *De Iure Parochorum*, n. 47, p. 45.

parted throughout the octave of Easter.[14] Under the law of the Code, however, the time for the solemn blessing of homes is to be determined by local custom.[15]

May the pastor licitly bestow this blessing even on the homes of non-Catholics in his parish? Canon 1149 expressly concedes that blessings may be granted to non-Catholics with a view to obtaining for them the light of faith together with bodily health, or at least the light of faith, provided that there be no ecclesiastical prohibition to the contrary. Hence it is evident that the blessing of a home, when performed *privately,* with all danger of scandal being avoided, may be legitimately imparted in favor of non-Catholics.[16] It is the opinion of the writer, however, that the blessing of Holy Saturday may not be bestowed on the homes of non-Catholics, in view of an ecclesiastical prohibition to the contrary. In its instruction of June 22, 1859, the Sacred Congregation of the Holy Office barred non-Catholics from participation in certain sacramentals which, because of their public nature, might give the impression that non-Catholics and Catholics were linked together in the common bond of faith.[17] Because the blessing of homes on Holy Saturday partakes of a solemn and public nature, the writer includes it among those sacramentals which may convey a false impression when they are bestowed in favor of non-Catholics.

Section 3. THE BLESSING OF THE BAPTISMAL FONT ON HOLY SATURDAY

Unlike the blessing of homes, the blessing of the baptismal font on Holy Saturday is reserved to the pastor with one important restriction. It is within the pastor's competence to bless the font on Holy Saturday, provided that the parish church be not united with a collegiate chapter which has reserved to itself the right to perform the sacred functions of Holy Week, including the blessing of the font.[18] In the latter event the blessing of the

[14] S. R. C., *Isclana,* 20 nov. 1885, ad 2—*Fontes,* n. 6168; 7 mart. 1903—*Fontes,* n. 6323.

[15] Canon 462, 6º.

[16] Cf. *ER,* XCI (1934), 315.

[17] *Fontes,* n. 952.

[18] Canons 462, 7º, and 415, §1, 3º. Cf. Cappello, *Summa,* II, n. 516; Vermeersch-Creusen, *Epitome,* I, n. 548, p. 398.

font will be performed by the ranking dignitary of the chapter, not by the parochial vicar.[19]

Under the former law it was possible for one parish to maintain exclusive baptismal rights over one or more parishes, so that the filial parishes were prevented from having their own font, and their pastors were obliged to assist at the blessing of the font in the mother parish.[20] The law of the Code, however, prescribes that every parish possess its own baptismal font, notwithstanding any existing custom or statute to the contrary.[21] Hence every pastor, with the possible exception of the aforementioned parochial vicar, will have the right and the corresponding duty to bless the baptismal font on Holy Saturday. Under the present law it is also possible for the local ordinary to permit or even to command that a font be erected in a church which is not a parish church, or even in a public oratory.[22] The right to bless such a "non-parochial" font belongs to the rector of the church or of the public oratory.

In canon 462, 7°, there is no mention of the blessing of the baptismal font on the vigil of Pentecost, yet liturgical law prescribes that it be blessed on that day as well as on Holy Saturday.[23] Because of the silence of canon 462, 7°, the question may arise whether the blessing of the font on the vigil of Pentecost, like the blessing of the font on Holy Saturday, be a reserved parochial function. The affirmative view is solidly probable, since it is based on the argument from the analogy of law, as well as on the general norm: "canones qui ius vetus ex integro referunt, ex veteris iuris auctoritate . . . sunt aestimandi." [24] Moreover,

[19] S. R. C., *Drepanen.*, 5 iul. 1871, ad 1—*Fontes,* n. 6040.

[20] S. R. C., *Lucana,* 12 apr. 1755—*DA,* n. 2436; S. C. C., *Utinen.,* 13 ian. 1899—*ASS,* XXXI (1898-1899), 541; *Lucana et Ariminen.,* 27 apr. 1907—*Thesaurus,* CLXVI (1907), 211; *Cremonen.,* 10 iun. 1922—*AAS,* XV (1923), 226; "Le Sacrament de Baptême," *Analecta Iuris Pontificii,* VIII (1866), 1574.

[21] Canon 774, §1.

[22] Canon 774, §2.

[23] *Rituale Romanum,* tit. 2, c. 1, *de sacramento baptismi rite administrando,* n. 5; S. C. C., *Utinen.,* 13 ian. 1899—*ASS,* XV (1923), 226.

[24] Canon 6, 2°. Cf. S. C. C., *Cremonen.,* 10 iun. 1922—*AAS,* XV (1923), 225-227; *Jus Pontificium,* VIII (1928), 155; Cocchi, *Commentarium,* III, n. 341, p. 413; Fanfani, *De Iure Parochorum,* n. 47, p. 45.

since the same kind of obligation obtains in the two cases, it is apparent that also the same kind of right should be acknowledged as occasioned by the obligation.

Section 4. THE BESTOWAL OF SOLEMN BLESSINGS OUTSIDE THE CHURCH

Besides the blessing of homes and the blessing of the baptismal font, the pastor also enjoys exclusive competence over all solemn blessings ("*benedictiones . . . cum pompa et solemnitate*") bestowed within the parish limits, provided that they are imparted outside a church.[25] If the solemn blessing is bestowed inside a church or public oratory, the right to bestow it belongs to the rector or chaplain of the church or oratory. If on the other hand the blessing is bestowed outside a church but in a private manner, any priest, whether secular or religious, may impart it without violating in any way the right of the pastor.[26]

It is necessary therefore to determine the precise nature of a solemn blessing in order to decide which specific blessings are reserved to the pastor's exclusive competence. Certainly a blessing may be called solemn if it is imparted in the presence of a great throng of people.[27] If the minister is assisted by other clerics, or if the blessing is accompanied with the ringing of bells or the use of incense, authors maintain that such circumstances would constitute a solemn blessing.[28] On the other hand, if the blessing is imparted by a priest in the absence of any notable concourse of people, such a blessing would be of a private nature, and consequently would not call for the offices of the pastor.[29]

When the blessing is imparted by any priest inside a church, it may be surrounded with the utmost solemnity, and yet be exercised without any infringement of the pastor's right. Thus

---

[25] Canon 462, 7°.

[26] S. R. C., 13 iun. 1893—*DA,* n. 3801; Cappello, *Summa,* II, n. 518; Vermeersch-Creusen, *Epitome,* I, n. 548, p. 399.

[27] Cf. Coronata, *Institutiones Iuris Canonici,* II, n. 481, p. 563, nota 4.

[28] Coronata, *loc. cit.;* Cappello, *Summa,* II, n. 518; Cocchi, *Commentarium,* III, n. 341, p. 414.

[29] Cf. S. R. C., 13 iun. 1893, ad 6 (*DA,* n. 3801), wherein the Sacred Congregation declared that any priest could bless the fields, livestock and similar objects "*ritu privato.*"

the blessing of palms, of ashes, of candles, of throats, as also the blessing of women after childbirth may be freely performed in any church or public oratory, without the need of obtaining the permission of the local pastor, unless there should be a particular law to the contrary.[30] It is to be noted, finally, that the bestowal of solemn blessings outside a church, like the blessing of the baptismal font, is conditionally reserved to the pastor. If the parish is united with a cathedral or collegiate chapter, and if the chapter has reserved this function to itself, the bestowal of solemn blessings outside the church will pertain, not to the parochial vicar, but to the ranking dignitary of the chapter.[31]

Article 2. *The Conducting of Public Processions outside the Church*

Section 1. SACRED PROCESSIONS IN GENERAL

A sacred procession may be defined as a solemn form of liturgical worship whereby the faithful, under the leadership of the clergy, proceed in an orderly fashion from sacred place to sacred place for the purpose of arousing the devotion of the faithful and of accomplishing the four ends to which all prayer is ordained.[32] A sacred procession is a corporate prayer in which the whole man participates; it is a sensible expression of man's faith and love of God. A true ecclesiastical procession must be composed of members of the faithful and must be carried out under the leadership of the clergy. If the procession is conducted along the public thoroughfares, it is public; on the other hand, if it is restricted to the interior of a church, or of a cloister, or if it be confined to the immediate vicinity thereof, the procession is considered to be of a private nature.[33]

---

[30] Cf. Sipos, *Enchiridion Iuris Canonici* (4. ed., Pécs: Ex Typographia "Haladas R. T.," 1940), p. 316; Claeys Boúúaert-Simenon, *Manuale Juris Canonici,* I, n. 570, p. 315.

[31] Cf. Cappello, *Summa,* II, n. 518, p. 64; Oesterle, *Praelectiones Iuris Canonici,* I (Romae: In Collegio S. Anselmi, 1931), 217.

[32] Canon 1290, §1. Cf. Coronata, *Institutiones Iuris Canonici,* II, n. 866; Woywod, "Law of the Code on Divine Cult," *The Homiletic and Pastoral Review,* XXVII (1926-1927), 390-394.

[33] Cf. Beste, *Introductio in Codicem,* p. 635; Cappello, *Summa,* II, n. 517;

With reference to the note of its origin, a procession may be *ordinary* or *extraordinary*. The former is that type of procession which is annually conducted on certain determined feasts, as prescribed in the liturgical books of the Church, or by particular custom; the extraordinary procession is one which is conducted outside these stated times, for some public reason of a transitory nature, as, for example, in time of war, of plague, or of famine.[34] Apart from the possible additions they may obtain as the result of some particular law, the ordinary processions are appointed for the following days: the feast of the Purification of the Blessed Virgin, Palm Sunday, the feast of St. Mark, the three Rogation Days immediately preceding Ascension Thursday, and Corpus Christi.[35]

Special provisions are enacted in the common law regarding the procession of Corpus Christi. On that day, if circumstances will permit and there be no immemorial custom to the contrary, only one solemn procession in any given locality is to be held from the most venerable church of the community, in which all the clergy, all the male religious, even exempt, as well as all lay confraternities are to participate. Exception is made only for the religious of the strictly contemplative orders and for those who live more than two miles outside the town or city.[36] The

---

Berutti, *Institutiones Iuris Canonici* (6 vols., Vol. IV, Taurini: Marietti, 1940), IV, n. 85, p. 284. In a certain decision of the Roman Rota (*Tarentin.*, 3 febr. 1922, coram F. Parillo—*AAS,* XIV [1922], 397), a procession which is conducted by the faithful and the clergy of a church is called a *particular* or a *private* procession, reference being made to Wernz, who in his *Ius Decretalium* (Vol. II, tit. 21, n. 656, II) defines a *public* procession as one which is composed of the entire clergy and people of a city or town. This notion of a public procession in no way conforms to the concept embodied in canon 462, 7°, for if every pastor has the right to conduct public processions, then public processions must be possible on a parochial scale, and the distinction between public and private procession must consist in whether or not the procession is conducted through the streets of the town or on the public highways.

[34] Canon 1290, §2.

[35] *Rituale Romanum,* tit. 9, c. 1, *de processionibus,* n. 8.

[36] Canon 1291, §1.

other churches in the community may conduct their individual processions during the octave of the feast.[37]

It pertains to the office of the local ordinary to supervise and enact specific regulations for the good order of all possessions conducted within the diocese.[38] A pastor may not inaugurate a new procession, nor may he transfer or abolish a traditional procession, without the permission of the local ordinary.[39] With proper exception made for the procession during the octave of Corpus Christi, religious (including exempt religious) may not conduct a procession outside their church or cloister without the permission of the local ordinary.[40]

Section 2. SACRED PROCESSIONS AS A RESERVED PAROCHIAL FUNCTION

Among the functions which the Code reserves to pastors, there is included the right to conduct public processions outside the church.[41] To conduct a procession is a purely honorary prerogative; it includes the right to have one's own cross carried at the head of the procession, and the right to determine the route of march.[42] When the Code was promulgated, a question arose concerning the interpretation of the phrase "*extra ecclesiam.*" Did it point to only those processions which started at the parish church, or did it refer also to those which may proceed from other churches lying within the parochial limits, even though such churches be not filial churches and have their own rector? On November 12, 1922, the Pontifical Commission for the Interpretation of the Code answered this question in the negative to the first part, and in the affirmative to the second part, exception being made only for the procession within the octave of Corpus Christi.[43]

---

[37] Canon 1291, §2.

[38] Canon 1295.

[39] Canon 1294, §1.

[40] Canon 1293. Cf. Regatillo, *Ius Sacramentarium,* I, n. 380.

[41] Canon 462, 7o.

[42] Cf. *Jus Pontificium,* VIII (1928), 154.

[43] Resp. ad 1—*AAS,* XIV (1922), 661. This response was not to be construed as admitting any infringement upon the rector's right to perform non-reserved ecclesiastical functions within the church, as expressed in canon 482.

Some doubt still lingered, however, concerning the precise extent of the pastor's prerogative. Did his right to lead processions extend even to the processions of exempt religious when conducted outside their churches and cloisters? Again the Pontifical Commission replied in the affirmative, due exception being made for the procession within the octave of Corpus Christi.[44]

The right of the pastor to conduct public processions must therefore be understood in its widest sense to include all public processions, whether ordinary or extraordinary, held within the parish limits, with the sole exception of the procession which religious and rectors of churches have a right to conduct during the octave of Corpus Christi.[45] As it has already been stated, the writer follows Beste, Cappello and Berutti in regarding as a public procession any procession which is conducted along the public thoroughfares of the community. If a procession is confined within the church, or if it be restricted to the cloister, the courtyard or the immediate vicinity of the church or the cloister, it is not public, and hence is not subject to the honorary primacy of the local pastor. Indeed, a procession may even venture into the streets immediately adjacent to the walls of the church and still remain a private procession.[46]

Like the blessing of the font and the solemn blessings bestowed outside a church, the conducting of public processions is conditionally reserved to pastors. The condition is that the parish church be not also a capitular church, or, if it be such, that the cathedral or the collegiate chapter does not, by a specially reserved

---

[44] Resp. 10 nov. 1925, ad 5—*AAS*, XVII (1925), 582.

[45] By apostolic privilege, the Dominicans may also conduct a public procession on the first Sunday of October—Prümmer, *Manuale Iuris Canonici*, n. 395.

[46] "Elocutio: *Claustra*, late sumenda est, ut non tantum ecclesias, sed et hortum vel fundum circumstantem Domui religiosae comprehendat, etsi de non exemptis agatur. Immo in hac re antiquam interpretationem retinere licet, e qua Religiosi possunt processionem ducere etiam per contiguam viam ecclesiae, si claustra non habeant"—Schaefer, *De Religiosis ad normam Codicis Iuris Canonici*, n. 491, p. 890. For the pre-Code law in this matter, cf. S. R. C., *Hispalen.*, 26 febr. 1628—*DAG*, n. 723; *Limana*, 15 dec. 1632—*DAG*, n. 970; *decr. gen.*, 28 sept. 1658—*Fontes*, n. 5508.

right, perform this function. In such a case the conducting of public processions would pertain to the ranking dignitary of the chapter, rather than to the parochial vicar.[47]

---

[47] Canon 462, 7°, and 415, §1, 3°. Cf. Cappello, *Summa,* n. 517; Oesterle, *Praelectiones Iuris Canonici,* I, 217.

CONCLUSIONS

1. It is the first and most fundamental conclusion of the writer that the statement of Coronata [1] that the Code generally does not look with favor on reserved parochial functions cannot be substantiated. From the very beginning of the parochial system pastors have been accorded certain special prerogatives in connection with their office. In no way can it be said that the Code has departed from the traditional jurisprudence and legislation regarding parochial functions. Efforts to prune abuses must not be misinterpreted as disapproval of the institution.

2. The origin of reserved parochial functions may be traced to two distinct sources. The earlier of these two sources—the "*iura paroecialia*"—had become crystallized by the time of the Council of Trent and pertained more to the efficiency of the parochial office than to its honor and dignity. The later source—"*functiones parochiales*"—was not so clearly defined in character and evolved only after centuries of controversy between pastors on the one hand and confraternities, third orders and religious communities on the other hand.

3. The legislation of the Code governing reserved parochial functions is enacted with the explicit condition: "*nisi aliud iure caveatur.*" In virtue of this clause freedom is accorded to particular law to amend the provisions of the Code in the matter of reserved parochial functions, provided that the particular law does not conflict with any other prescriptions of the common law.

4. According to the common law, solemn baptism is a function which is reserved to the competence of the proper pastor. In the case of adult converts, however, particular custom or statute may legitimately accord this right to the priest who imparted the instructions.

5. Since the practice of having general or solemn Communions is no longer approved, the reservation to pastors of the solemn first Communion cannot be regarded as commendable.

[1] *Institutiones Iuris Canonici,* I, n. 481, nota 4.

6. The right to assist at mixed marriages belongs to the pastor of the bride, even though she be a non-Catholic. Here again local custom and diocesan statute may overrule the common law.

7. As a reserved parochial function, the administration of Holy Viaticum is restricted to that Communion which is prescribed by divine as well as ecclesiastical law when one falls into serious danger of death, and does not extend to other Communions which one receives out of devotion while still seriously ill.

8. The right to select the church for one's funeral and the cemetery for one's burial is more fundamental than the right of one's proper pastor to conduct the funeral, and when the former is duly exercised, it takes precedence over the latter.

BIBLIOGRAPHY

SOURCES

Acta Apostolicae Sedis, Commentarium Officiale, Romae, 1909—.

Acta Sanctae Sedis, 41 vols., Rómae, 1865–1908.

Acta Ecclesiae Mediolanensis, cura et studio A. Ratti, 3 vols. in 2, Mediolani, 1890–1892.

Bouscaren, T. Lincoln, *The Canon Law Digest,* 2 vols., Milwaukee: Bruce, 1934, 1943.

Bruns, Hermann Theodor, *Canones Apostolorum et Conciliorŭm Saeculorum IV–VII,* 2 vols., Berolini, 1839.

Bullarum Diplomatum et Privilegiorum Sanctorum Pontificum Taurinensis Editio, 24 vols. et Appendix, Augustae Taurinorum, 1857–1872.

Canones et Decreta Sacrosancti Oecumenici Concilii Tridentini, Editio novissima ad Fidem Optimorum Exemplarium Castigate Impressa (XIX reimpressio stereotypa), Taurini, 1913.

Codicis Iuris Canonici Fontes cura Emi Petri Card. Gasparri editi, 9 vols., Romae (later Civitate Vaticana): Typis Polyglottis Vaticanis, 1923–1939. (Vols. VII–IX, ed. cura et studio Emi Iustiniani Serédi).

Collectanea S. Congregationis de Propraganda Fide, 2 vols., Romae: Typographia Polyglotta, S. C. de Propaganda Fide, 1907.

Concilii Plenarii Baltimorensis Secundi Acta et Decreta, 2. ed., Baltimore, 1880.

Corpus Iuris Canonici, Editio Lipsiensis II (Richter-Friedberg), 2 vols., Lipsiae, 1879–1881.

Decreta Authentica Congregationis Sacrorum Rituum, 6 vols., Romae: Ex Typographia Polyglotta, 1898–1927.

Decreta Authentica Congregationis Sacrorum Rituum ex actis eiusdem collecta, cura et studio Aloisii Gardellini, 3. ed., 5 vols., Romae, 1856–1879.

Hardouin, Jean, *Acta Conciliorum et Epistolae Decretales ac Constitutiones Summorum Pontificum,* 12 vols., Parisiis, 1714–1715.

Hefele, Carolus-Leclercq, Henricus, *Histoire des Conciles,* 10 vols. in 19, Paris: Letouzey et Ané, 1907–1938.

Jaffé, Philippus, *Regesta Pontificum Romanorum ab condita Ecclesia ad annum post Christum natum MCXCVIII* (2. ed. [Kaltenbrunner, Ewald, Loewenfeld]), 2 vols. in 1, Lipsiae, 1885–1888.

Labbé, P-Cossart, G., *Sacrosancta Concilia ad regiam editionem exacta,* 15 vols. in 16, Parisiis, 1671–1674.

Langlois, E., *Les Registres de Nicolas IV, Bibliotheque des Écoles francaises d'Athènes et de Rome,* 2 ser., t. 5, Paris, 1886.

Mollat, G., *Jean XXII, Lettres Communes, Bibliotheque des Écoles francaises d'Athènes et de Rome,* 14 vols. in 11, Paris, E. DeBoccard, 1904–1935.

Mansi, J. D., *Sacrorum Conciliorum Nova et Amplissima Collectio,* 53 vols. in 60, Parisiis, 1901–1927.

Missale Romanum, Editio III juxta Typicam Vaticanam, Neo Eboraci: Benziger Brothers, 1944.

Monumenta Germaniae Historica, 188 vols. incomplete, Hannoverae, 1826—;
Leges, T. I, ed. G. H. Pertz, 1835; T. II, ed. G. H. Pertz, 1837;
Leges in 4, Sectio II (*Capitularia Regum Francorum*), T. I, ed. A. Boretius, 1883; Sectio III (*Concilia*), T. I, ed. F. Maassen, 1893; T. II, ed. A. Werminghoff, 1906–1908; Sectio IV (*Constitutiones*), T. I, ed. L. Weiland, 1893;
Epistolae, 7 vols., 1887–1928; T. I, pars II, ed. P. Ewald, 1891.

Potthast, A., *Regesta Pontificum Romanorum inde ab anno post Christum natum MCXCVIII ad annum MCCCIV,* 2 vols., Berolini, 1874–1875.

Rituale Romanum, Editio juxta Typicam Vaticanam, Neo Eboraci: Benziger Brothers, 1944.

Schroeder, H. J., *Disciplinary Decrees of the General Councils, Text, Translation and Commentary,* St. Louis: Herder, 1937.

Synodus Dioecesana Fargensis Prima, Milwaukee: Bruce, 1941.

Thesaurus Resolutionum Sacrae Congregationis Concilii, 167 vols., Romae, 1718–1908.

AUTHORS

Aichner, S., *Compendium Juris Ecclesiastici,* 6. ed., Brixinae, 1887.

Augustine, Charles, *A Commentary on the New Code of Canon Law,* 8 vols., Vol. IV, 6. ed., St. Louis: Herder & Co., 1931.

Ayrinhac, H. A., *Administrative Legislation in the New Code of Canon Law,* New York: Longmans, Green & Co., 1930.

———, *Marriage Legislation in the New Code of Canon Law,* revised and enlarged by P. J. Lydon, New York: Benziger Brothers, 1932.

Barbosa, A., *De Officio et Potestate Parochi Descriptio,* ed. U. Giraldi S. Cajetano, Romae, 1774.

———, *Summa Apostolicarum Decisionum extra Ius Commune Vagantium,* Lugduni, 1645.

Studies in Medieval History, edited by Geoffrey Barraclough, *Medieval Germany,* 911–1250, Vol. I (Introduction); Vol. II (Essays), Oxford: Blackwell and Mott, Ltd., 1938.

Benedictus XIV, *De Synodo Dioecesana,* 2 vols., Romae, 1806.

———, *Institutiones Ecclesiasticae,* Prati, 1844.

Bernardus Papiensis, *Summa Decretalium,* ed. E. A. T. Laspeyres, Ratisbonae, 1860.

Berutti, C., *Institutiones Iuris Canonici,* 6 vols., Vol. IV, Taurini: Marietti, 1940.

Beste, *Introductio in Codicem,* 2. ed., Collegeville, Minn.: St. John's Abbey Press, 1944.

Blat, Albertus, *Commentarium Textus Codicis Iuris Canonici,* 5 vols. in 7, Vol. II (*De Personis*), Romae: Ex Typographia Pontificia in Instituto Pii X, 1923; Vol. II, pars I (*De Personis*), 1923; Vol, III, pars I (*De Sacramentis*), 1924.

Bouis, Dominicus, *Tractatus de Episcopo,* 2. ed., 2 vols. in 1, Parisiis, 1873.

———, *Tractatus de Parocho,* 3. ed., Parisiis, 1880.

Bouscaren, T.,-Ellis, A., *Canon Law, A Text and Commentary,* Milwaukee: Bruce, 1946.

Bouuaert, F. Claeys-Simenon, G., *Manuale Juris Canonici,* 3 vols., Vol. I and III, 3. ed., Vol. 11, 1. ed., Gandae et Leodii: Dessain, 1930–1931.

Cappello, F. M., *Summa Iuris Canonici,* 3 vols., Vol. I, II, 3. ed., Romae: Universitas Gregoriana, 1938–1939.

———, *Tractatus Canonico-Moralis de Sacramentis,* 3 vols. in 6, Vol. I, 4. ed., Romae: Marietti, 1945; Vol. II, pars III, 1935; Vol. III, partes I et II, 4. ed., 1939.

Carberry, J., *The Juridical Form of Marriage,* The Catholic University of America Canon Law Studies, n. 84, Washington, D. C.: The Catholic University of America, 1934.

Chelodi, Ioannes, *Ius de Personis,* 3 ed., curavit P. Ciprotti, Trento: Libreria Moderna Edititrice, 1942.

———, *Ius Matrimoniale iuxta Codicem,* 3. ed., Tridenti: Tridentum, 1921.

Cicognani, Amleto, *Canon Law,* trans. by J. O'Hara and F. Brennan, Philadelphia: The Dolphin Press, 1934.

Cocchi, Guidus, *Commentarium in Codicem Iuris Canonici,* 8 vols. in 5, Vol. V (Lib. III, *De Rebus;* Pars II, *De Locis et temporibus* sacris; Pars III, *De cultu divino*), 4. ed., Taurinorum Augustae: Marietti, 1938.

Coronata, Matthaeus Conte a, *De Locis et Temporibus Sacris,* Augustae Taurinorum: Marietti, 1922.

———, *Institutiones Iuris Canonici,* 5 vols., Vols. I–II, 2. ed., 1939; Vol. III, 2. ed., 1941; Vol. IV, 2. ed., 1945; Vol. V, 1936, Taurini: Marietti.

———, *Tractatus Canonicus de Sacramentis,* 3 vols., Romae; Marietti, 1943–1946.

Costello, J., *Domicile and Quasi-Domicile,* The Catholic University of America Canon Law Studies, n. 60, Washington, D. C.: The Catholic University of America, 1930.

Creusen, J., *Religious Men and Women in the Code,* 4. English ed. revised and edited to conform with the 5. French ed. by A. Ellis, Milwaukee: 1940.

De Becker, Iulius, *De Matrimonio Praelectiones Canonicae,* ed. nova, Lovanii: Fr. Ceuterick, 1931.

De Bonis, J., *De Oratoriis Publicis,* Mediolani, 1761.

De Fargna, F., *Commentaria in Singulos Canones de Jure Patronatus,* 3 vols., Montisfalisci, 1717–1719.

De Meester, A., *Juris Canonici et Juris Canonico-Civilis Compendium,* nova editio, 3 vols. in 4, Brugis, 1921–1928.

De Smet, Al., *Tractatus Theologico-canonicus de Sponsalibus et Matrimonio,* 4. ed., Brugis: Car. Beyaert, 1927.

Duchesne, Louis, *Le Liber Pontificalis Texte, Introduction et Commentaire,* 2 vols., Parisiis, 1886–1892.

Engel, L., *Collegium Universi Iuris Canonici,* ed. nona; post omnes alias recognita et locupleta; cui nunc primum adjectae sunt annotationes Caspari Barthel, Beneventi, 1760.

Fanfani, L., *De Iure Parochorum,* Romae: Marietti, 1924.

Feldhaus, A. H., *Oratories,* The Catholic University of America Canon Law Studies, n. 42, Washington, D. C.: The Catholic University of America, 1927.

Ferraris, Lucius, *Prompta Bibliotheca Canonica, Iuridica, Moralis, Theologica, necnon Ascetica, Polemica, Rubricistica, Historica,* ed. noviss., 9 vols., Romae, 1885–1899.

Ferry, W., *Stole Fees,* The Catholic University of America Canon Law Studies, n. 59, Washington, D. C.: The Catholic University of America, 1930.

Fournier, P.–LeBras, G., *Histoire des Collections Canoniques en Occident,* 2 vols., Paris, Recueil Sirey, 1931.

Galtier, P., *L'Eglise et la Remission des Pêches aux Premiers Siècles,* Paris: G. Beauchesne, 1932.

Gasparri, Petrus, *Tractatus canonicus de matrimonio,* ed. nova, 2 vols. in 1, Typis Polyglottis Vaticanis, 1932.

———, *Tractatus Canonicus de Sanctissima Eucharistia,* 2 vols., Parisiis, 1897.

Gasquet, F., *Parish Life in Medieval England,* New York: Benziger Brothers, 1906.

Gennari, C., *Quistioni Canoniche,* 2. ed., Roma, 1908.

Hinschius, Paul, *Das Kirchenrecht der Katholiken und Protestanten in Deutschland,* 6 vols., Berlin, 1869–1897.

Hostiensis, Cardinalis (Henricus de Segusia), *Commentaria in Quinque Libros Decretalium,* 3 vols., Venetiis, 1581.

Imbart de la Tour, P., *De Ecclesiis Rusticanis Aetate Carolingica,* Burgdigalae, 1890.

Jorio, D., *La Communione agl' Infermi,* Roma: Pustet, 1931.

Kilker, A. J., *Extreme Unction,* The Catholic University of America Canon Law Studies, n. 32, Washington, D. C.: The Catholic University of America, 1926.

Lehmkuhl, A., *Theologia Moralis,* 2 vols., 9. ed., Friburgi Brisgoviae, 1898.

Many, S., *De Sacra Ordinatione,* Parisiis, 1905.

———, *Praelectiones Canonicae de Locis Sacris,* Parisiis, 1904.

Maroto, Philippus, *Institutiones Iuris Canonici,* 2 vols., Vol. I, 3. ed., 1921; Vol. II, 1919, Romae: Apud Commentarium pro Religiosis.

Merkelbach, B. H., *Summa Theologiae Moralis,* 3. ed., 3 vols., Parisiis: Desclee, de Brouwer et Cie, 1939.

Michiels, G., *Normae Generales Juris Canonici,* 2 vols., Lublin: Universitas Catholica, 1929.

——, *Principia Generalia de Personis in Ecclesia,* Lublin: Universitas Catholica, 1932.

Migne, J. P., *Patrologiae Cursus Completus, Series Latina,* 221 vols., Parisiis, 1844–1864.

——, *Series Graeca,* 161 vols., Parisiis, 1856–1866.

Monacelli, Fr., *Formularium Legale Practicum Fori Ecclesiastici,* 3. ed., 4 vols. in 3, Romae, 1844.

Neuberger, N., *Canon 6, or the Relation of the Codex Iuris Canonici to the Preceding Legislation,* The Catholic University of America Canon Law Studies, n. 44, Washington, D. C.: The Catholic University of America, 1927.

Noldin, H.-Schmitt, A., *Summa Theologiae Moralis,* 26. ed., 3 vols., Ratisbonae: Pustet, 1940.

O'Brien, J., *The Exemption of Religious in Church Law,* Milwaukee: Bruce, 1942.

Oesterle, G., *Praelectiones Iuris Canonici,* Vol. I, Romae: In Collegio S. Anselmi, 1931.

Ojetti, B., *Commentarium in Codicem Iuris Canonici,* 4 vols., Romae: Universitas Gregoriana, 1927–1931.

Panormitanus, Abbas (Nicolaus de Tudeschis), *Commentaria super quinque Libros Decretalium,* 5 vols., Lugduni, 1547.

Payen, G., *De Matrimonio in Missionibus ac potissimum in Sinis Tractatus Practicus et Casus,* 2. ed., 3 vols., Zi-ka-wei: In Typographia T'ou-se-we, 1935–1936.

Petit, G., *La Part Paroissiale ou Quarte Funéraire,* Les Theses Canoniques de Laval, Thèse n. 5, Québec: Université Laval, 1946.

Petrovits, J., *The New Church Law On Matrimony,* The Catholic University of America Canon Law Studies, n. 6, Washington, D. C.: The Catholic University of America, 1919.

Pilatus, Leopold Frieherr von, *Origines Iuris Pontificii ad Carolum Sextum,* Tridenti, 1739.

Pirhing, E., *Ius Canonicum Nova Methodo Explicatum,* 5 vols., Dilingae, 1674–1678.

Poschmann, B., *Die abendländische Kirchenbusse im Ausgang des christlichen Altertums,* München, J. Kösel-F. Pustet, 1928.

Prümmer, D., *Manuale Iuris Canonici,* 6. ed., Friburgi Brisgoviae: Herder, 1933.

——, *Manuale Theologiae Moralis,* 3 vols., 3. ed., Friburgi Brisgoviae: Herder, 1923.

Realencyklopädie für protestantische Theologie und Kirche, 3. ed., 24 vols., Leipzig, 1890–1913.

Regatillo, E., *Ius Sacramentarium,* 2 vols., Santander: Sal Terrae, 1945–1946.

Reiffenstuel, Anacletus, *Ius Canonicum Universum,* 5 vols. in 6, Romae, 1831-1834.

Roberts, J., *The Banns of Marriage,* The Catholic University of America Canon Law Studies, n. 64, Washington, D. C.: The Catholic University of America, 1931.

Rossi, J., *De Matrimonii Celebratione iuxta Codicem Iuris Canonici,* Romae: Pustet, 1924.

Rossi, G., *La "Sepultura Ecclesiastica" e L' "Ius Funerum" nel Diritto Canonico,* Bergamo: Libreria Vescovile Editrice, 1920.

Rufinus, *Summa Decretorum,* ed. H. Singer, Paderborn, 1902.

Sägmüller, J. B., *Lehrbuch des katholischen Kirchenrechts,* 2 vols., 3. ed., Freiburg im Breisgau: Herder, 1914.

Santi, Franciscus, *Praelectiones Iuris Canonici,* editio quarta emendata et recentissimis decretis accommodata cura Martini Leitner, 5 vols., Ratisbonae, 1903–1905.

Schaefer, T., *De Religiosis ad Normam Codicis Iuris Canonici,* 3. ed., Romae: S. A. L. E. R., 1940.

———, *Die Kirchenämter nach dem Codex Iuris Canonici,* II Band, Pfarre und Pfarrvikare, Erste und zweite Auflage, Münster i. W.; Verlag der Aschendorffen Verlagsbuchhandlung, 1922.

Schmalzgrueber, Franciscus, *Ius Ecclesiasticum Universum,* 5 vols. in 12, Romae, 1843–1845.

Shuhler, R., *Privileges of Regulars to Absolve and Dispense,* The Catholic University of America Canon Law Studies, n. 186, Washington, D. C.: The Catholic University of America Press, 1943.

Sipos, S., *Enchiridion Iuris Canonici,* 4. ed., Pécs: Ex Typographia "Haladas R.T.," 1940.

Soglia, J., *Institutiones Juris Privati Ecclesiastici,* 2. ed., Parisiis, 1842.

Tachy, A., *Traité des Confreries et des Ouvres Pies,* 2. ed., Langres, 1898.

Thomassinus, Ludovicus, *Vetus et Nova Ecclesiae Disciplina,* 3 vols., Parisiis, 1688.

Toso, A., *Ad Codicem Iuris Canonici . . . Commentaria Minora,* 5 vols., Romae: Marietti, 1920–1927.

Van Hove, A., *Commentarium Lovaniense in Codicem Iuris Canonici,* Vol. I, tom. 1, *Prolegomena ad Codicem Iuris Canonici,* 2. ed., Mechliniae et Romae: Dessain, 1945; Vol. I, tom. 2, *De Legibus Ecclesiasticis,* 1930; Vol. I, tom. 3, *De Temporis Supputatione,* 1933.

Van Espen, Z. Bernardus, *Ius Ecclesiasticum Universum,* 10 vols., Venetiis, 1769.

Vermeersch, A.–Creusen, J., *Epitome Iuris Canonici,* 3 vols., Vol. I, 6. ed., Romae: Dessain, 1937; Vol. II, 6. ed., 1940.

Vlaming, Th. M., *Praelectiones Iuris Matrimonii,* 3. ed., 2 vols., Bussum in Hollandia: Sumptibus Societatis Editricis Anonymae, 1919, 1921.

Waldron, J., *The Minister of Baptism,* The Catholic University of America Canon Law Studies, n. 170, Washington, D. C.: The Catholic University of America Press, 1942.

Wernz, F. X., *Ius Decretalium,* 2. ed., 6 vols., Romae et Prati, 1906-1913.

Wernz, F. X.-Vidal, P., *Ius Canonicum,* 7 vols. in 8, Tom. II, 2. ed., 1928, Romae: Universitas Gregoriana; Tom. IV, Vol. 1, 1934; Tom. V, 3. ed., a P. Aguirre recognita, 1946.

Woywod, S., *A Practical Commentary on the Code of Canon Law,* 2 vols., ninth printing as edited by C. Smith, New York: J. Wagner, Inc., 1945.

ARTICLES

Berlière, U., "L'exercise du Ministère Paroissial par les Moines du XIIe au XVIIIe Siècle"—*Revue Bénédictine,* XXXIX (1927), 348-351.

Browe, P., "Die Kommunion in der Pfarrkirche"—*Zeitschrift für katholische Theologie,* LIII (1929), 477-516.

Christ, Joseph, "The Origin and Development of the Term 'Tituli'"—*The Jurist,* IV (1944), 101-123.

Clifford, J., "The Interpretation of Canon 1097"—*ER,* CVIII (1943), 122-125.

"De Baptismo in Paroecia Aliena"—*Jus Pontificium,* I-II (1921-1922), 109.

"Le Sacrament de Baptême"—*Analecta Iuris Pontificii,* VIII (1866), 1573-1604.

Palmer, P., "Jean Morin and the Problem of Private Penance"—*Theological Studies,* VI (1945), 317-357.

Piontek, C., "Equitable Practices under Canon 1097, § 2"—*The Jurist,* III (1943), 456-474.

Vermeersch, A., "'Ubi tumulus, ibi funus' . . . Axioma?"—*Periodica,* XVI (1927), 57-70.

Villien, A., "L'Ordination"—*Le Canoniste Contemporain,* XLV (1922), 388-399.

Woywod, S., "Rules for the Licit Assistance at Marriage"—*The Homiletic and Pastoral Review,* XXIV (1924). 1052-1059.

———, "The Law of the Code on Funerals"—*The Homiletic and Pastoral Review,* XXVI (1925-1926), 611-621.

———, "The Law of the Code on Divine Cult"—*The Homiletic and Pastoral Review,* XXVII (1926-1927), 387-394.

PERIODICALS

American Ecclesiastical Review, The, Vols. I-XXXII, Philadelphia, 1895-1905; from 1905: *The Ecclesiastical Review,* Vols. XXXIII—CIX, Philadelphia, 1905-1943; from 1944: *The American Ecclesiastical Review,* Washington, D. C., Vol. CX, 1944—

Analecta Iuris Pontificii, Romae, 1855-1869; Parisiis, 1872-1891.

Canoniste Contemporain, Le, Paris, 1878-1922; ab anno 1924-1926, *Le Canoniste.*
Homiletic and Pastoral Review, The, New York, 1900—
Irish Ecclesiastical Record, The, Dublin, 1864—
Jurist, The, Washington, D. C., 1941—
Jus Pontificium, Romae, 1921—
Periodica de Religiosis et Missionariis, Brugis, 1905-1919; *Periodica de Re Canonica et Morali utili praesertim Religiosis et Missionariis,* 1920-1927; *Periodica de Re Canonica, Morali, Liturgica,* 1927—
Revue Bénédictine, Abbaye de Maredsous, 1884—
Theological Studies, Woodstock, Md., 1940—
Zeitschrift für katholische Theologie, Innsbruck, 1877—

ABBREVIATIONS

AAS—Acta Apostolicae Sedis.
Acta et Decreta—Concilii Plenarii Baltimorensis Secundi Acta et Decreta.
AER—The American Ecclesiastical Review.
ASS—Acta Sanctae Sedis.
Bruns—*Canones Apostolorum et Conciliorum saec. IV–VII,* ed. Bruns.
Bull. Rom.—Bullarum Diplomatum et Privilegiorum Sanctorum Pontificum Taurinensis Editio.
DA—Decreta Authentica Congregationis Sacrorum Rituum.
DAG—Decreta Authentica Congregationis Sacrorum Rituum, cura et studio Aloisii Gardellini.
ER—The Ecclesiastical Review.
Fontes—Codicis Iuris Canonici Fontes cura . . . Gasparri editi.
Hardouin—*Acta Conciliorum, etc.*
JE—Jaffé, *Regesta Pontificum Romanorum* (edited by Ewald; for the years 590–882.
JK—Jaffé, *op. cit.* (edited by Kaltenbrunner; to the year 590).
JL—Jaffé, *op. cit.* (edited by Loewenfeld; for the years 882–1198).
Mansi—*Sacrorum Conciliorum Nova et Amplissima Collectio.*
MGH—Monumenta Germaniae Historica.
MPL—Migne, *Patrologia Latina.*
Periodica—Periodica de Re Morali, Canonica, Liturgica.
S.C.C.—Sacra Congregatio Concilii.
S.R.C.—Sacrorum Rituum Congretatio.
Thesaurus—Sacrae Congregationis Concilii Resolutiones.

INDEX

BIOGRAPHICAL NOTE

Bernard M. Kelly was born on May 7, 1918, at Providence, Rhode Island. He attended Blessed Sacrament Parochial School, LaSalle Academy and Providence College in Providence, Rhode Island. He pursued his studies for the Holy Priesthood in the Pontificio Seminario Romano Maggiore, Rome, Italy, and the Theological College of The Catholic University, Washington, D. C. He received the Licentiate in Sacred Theology from the Catholic University of America in May, 1944, and was ordained to the Holy Priesthood on June 3, 1944. In September, 1944, he enrolled in the School of Canon Law of the Catholic University of America, where he received the Degree of the Baccalaureate in Canon Law in May, 1945, and the Licentiate in Canon Law the following year.

CANON LAW STUDIES*

1. Freriks, Rev. Celestine A., C.PP.S., J.C.D., Religious Congregations in Their External Relations, 121 pp., 1916.
2. Galliher, Rev. Daniel M., O.P., J.C.D., Canonical Elections, 117 pp., 1917.
3. Borkowski, Rev. Aurelius L., O.F.M., J.C.D., De Confraternitatibus Ecclesiasticis, 136 pp., 1918.
4. Castillo, Rev. Cayo, J.C.D., Disertacion Historico-Canonica sobre la Potestad del Cabildo en Sede Vacante o Impedida del Vicario Capitular, 99 pp., 1919 (1918).
5. Kubelbeck, Rev. William J., S.T.B., J.C.D., The Sacred Penitentiaria and Its Relation to Faculties of Ordinaries and Priests, 129 pp., 1918.
6. Petrovits, Rev. Joseph J. C., S.T.D., J.C.D., The New Church Law on Matrimony, X-461 pp., 1919.
7. Hickey, Rev. John J., S.T.B., J.C.D., Irregularities and Simple Impediments in the New Code of Canon Law, 100 pp., 1920.
8. Klekotka, Rev. Peter J., S.T.B., J.C.D., Diocesan Consultors, 179 pp., 1920.
9. Wanenmacher, Rev. Francis, J.C.D., The Evidence in Ecclesiastical Procedure Affecting the Marriage Bond, 1920 (Printed 1935).
10. Golden, Rev. Henry Francis, J.C.D., Parochial Benefices in the New Code, IV-119 pp., 1921 (Printed 1925).
11. Koudelka, Rev. Charles J., J.C.D., Pastors, Their Rights and Duties According to the New Code of Canon Law, 211 pp., 1921.
12. Melo, Rev. Antonius, O.F.M., J.C.D., De Exemptione Regularium, X-188 pp., 1921.
13. Schaaf, Rev. Valentine Theodore, O.F.M., S.T.B., J.C.D., The Cloister, X-180 pp., 1921.
14. Burke, Rev. Thomas Joseph, S.T.D., J.C.D., Competence in Ecclesiastical Tribunals, IV-117 pp., 1922.
15. Leech, Rev. George Leo, J.C.D., A Comparative Study of the Constitution "Apostolicae Sedis" and the "Codex Juris Canonici," 179 pp., 1922.
16. Motry, Rev. Hubert Louis, S.T.D., J.C.D., Diocesan Faculties According to the Code of Canon Law, II-167 pp., 1922.
17. Murphy, Rev. George Lawrence, J.C.D., Delinquencies and Penalties in the Administration and the Reception of the Sacraments, IV-121 pp., 1923.

* From nn. 1-100 inclusive only nn. 7, 19, 25, 26, 31, 34, 44 and 51 are still obtainable. From n. 101 onward all numbers are available except the following: Nn. 101-114, 116, 118, 120, 122, 123, 162 and 198.

18. O'Reilly, Rev. John Anthony, S.T.B., J.C.D., Ecclesiastical Sepulture in the New Code of Canon Law, II-129 pp., 1923.
19. Michalicka, Rev. Wenceslas Cyrill, O.S.B., J.C.D., Judicial Procedure in Dismissal of Clerical Exempt Religious, 107 pp., 1923.
20. Dargin, Rev. Edward Vincent, S.T.B., J.C.D., Reserved Cases According to the Code of Canon Law, IV-103 pp., 1924.
21. Godfrey, Rev. John A., S.T.B., J.C.D., The Right of Patronage According to the Code of Canon Law, 153 pp., 1924.
22. Hagedorn, Rev. Francis Edward, J.C.D., General Legislation on Indulgences, II-154 pp., 1924.
23. King, Rev. James Ignatius, J.C.D., The Administration of the Sacraments to Dying Non-Catholics, V-141 pp., 1924.
24. Winslow, Rev. Francis Joseph, M.M., J.C.D., Vicars and Prefects Apostolic, IV-149 pp., 1924.
25. Correa, Rev. Jose Servelion, S.T.L., J.C.D., La Potestad Legislativa de la Iglesia Catolica, IV-127 pp., 1925.
26. Dugan, Rev. Henry Francis, A.M., J.C.D., The Judiciary Department of the Diocesan Curia, 87 pp., 1925.
27. Keller, Rev. Charles Frederick, S.T.B., J.C.D., Mass Stipends, 167 pp., 1925.
28. Paschang, Rev. John Linus, J.C.D., The Sacramentals According to the Code of Canon Law, 129 pp., 1925.
29. Piontek, Rev. Cyrillus, O.F.M., S.T.B., J.C.D., De Indulto Exclaustrationis necnon Saecularizationis, XIII-289 pp., 1925.
30. Kearney, Rev. Richard Joseph, S.T.B., J.C.D., Sponsors at Baptism According to the Code of Canon Law, IV-127 pp., 1925.
31. Bartlett, Rev. Chester Joseph, A.M., LL.B., J.C.D., The Tenure of Parochial Property in the United States of America, V-108 pp., 1926.
32. Kilker, Rev. Adrian Jerome, J.C.D., Extreme Unction, V-425 pp., 1926.
33. McCormick, Rev. Robert Emmett, J.C.D., Confessors of Religious, VIII-266 pp., 1926.
34. Miller, Rev. Newton Thomas, J.C.D., Founded Masses According to the Code of Canon Law, VII-93 pp., 1926.
35. Roelker, Rev. Edward G., S.T.D., J.C.D., Principles of Privilege According to the Code of Canon Law, XI-166 pp., 1926.
36. Bakalarczyk, Rev. Richardus, M.I.C., J.U.D., De Novitiatu, VIII-208 pp., 1927.
37. Pizzuti, Rev. Lawrence, O.F.M., J.U.L., De Parochis Religiosis, 1927. (Not Printed.)
38. Bliley, Rev. Nicholas Martin, O.S.B., J.C.D., Altars According to the Code of Canon Law, XIX-132 pp., 1927.
39. Brown, Mr. Brendan Francis, A.B., LL.M., J.U.D., The Canonical Juristic Personality with Special Reference to its Status in the United States of America, V-212 pp., 1927.

40. CAVANAUGH, REV. WILLIAM THOMAS, C.P., J.U.D., The Reservation of the Blessed Sacrament, VIII-101 pp., 1927.
41. DOHENY, REV. WILLIAM J., C.S.C., A.B., J.U.D., Church Property: Modes of Acquisition, X-118 pp., 1927.
42. FELDHAUS, REV. ALOYSIUS H., C.PP.S., J.C.D., Oratories, IX-141 pp., 1927.
43. KELLY, REV. JAMES PATRICK, A.B., J.C.D., The Jurisdiction of the Simple Confessor, X-208 pp., 1927.
44. NEUBERGER, REV. NICHOLAS J., J.C.D., Canon 6 or the Relation of the Codex Juris Canonici to the Preceding Legislation, V-95 pp., 1927.
45. O'KEEFE, REV. GERALD MICHAEL, J.C.D., Matrimonial Dispensations, Powers of Bishops, Priests, and Confessors, VIII-232 pp., 1927.
46. QUIGLEY, REV. JOSEPH A. M., A.B., J.C.D., Condemned Societies, 139 pp., 1927.
47. ZAPLOTNIK, REV. JOHANNES LEO, J.C.D., De Vicariis Foraneis, X-142 pp., 1927.
48. DUSKIE, REV. JOHN ALOYSIUS, A.B., J.C.D., The Canonical Status of the Orientals in the United States, VIII-196 pp., 1928.
49. HYLAND, REV. FRANCIS EDWARD, J.C.D., Excommunication, Its Nature, Historical Development and Effects, VIII-181 pp., 1928.
50. REINMANN, REV. GERALD JOSEPH, O.M.C., J.C.D., The Third Order Secular of Saint Francis, 201 pp., 1928.
51. SCHENK, REV. FRANCIS J., J.C.D., The Matrimonial Impediments of Mixed Religion and Disparity of Cult, XVI-318 pp., 1929.
52. COADY, REV. JOHN JOSEPH, S.T.D., J.U.D., A.M., The Appointment of Pastors, VIII-150 pp., 1929.
53. KAY, REV. THOMAS HENRY, J.C.D., Competence in Matrimonial Procedure, VIII-164 pp., 1929.
54. TURNER, REV. SIDNEY JOSEPH, C.P., J.U.D., The Vow of Poverty, XLIX-217 pp., 1929.
55. KEARNEY, REV. RAYMOND A., A.B., S.T.D., J.C.D., The Principles of Delegation, VII-149 pp., 1929.
56. CONRAN, REV. EDWARD JAMES, A.B., J.C.D., The Interdict, V-163 pp., 1930.
57. O'NEILL, REV. WILLIAM H., J.C.D., Papal Rescripts of Favor, VII-218 pp., 1930.
58. BASTNAGEL, REV. CLEMENT VINCENT, J.U.D., The Appointment of Parochial Adjutants and Assistants, XV-257 pp., 1930.
59. FERRY, REV. WILLIAM A., A.B., J.C.D., Stole Fees, V-136 pp., 1930.
60. COSTELLO, REV. JOHN MICHAEL, A.B., J.C.D., Domicile and Quasi-Domicile, VII-201 pp., 1930.
61. KREMER, REV. MICHAEL NICHOLAS, A.B., S.T.B., J.C.D., Church Support in the United States, VI-136 pp., 1930.
62. ANGULO, REV. LUIS, C.M., J.C.D., Legislation de la Iglesia sobre la intencion en la application de la Santa Misa, VII-104 pp., 1931.

63. Frey, Rev. Wolfgang Norbert, O.S.B., A.B., J.C.D., The Act of Religious Profession, VIII-174 pp., 1931.
64. Roberts, Rev. James Brendan, A.B., J.C.D., The Banns of Marriage, XIV-140 pp., 1931.
65. Ryder, Rev. Raymond Aloysius, A.B., J.C.D., Simony, IX-151 pp., 1931.
66. Campagna, Rev. Angelo, Ph.D., J.U.D., Il Vicario Generale del Vescovo, VII-205 pp., 1931.
67. Cox, Rev. Joseph Godfrey, A.B., J.C.D., The Administration of Seminaries, VI-124 pp., 1931.
68. Gregory, Rev. Donald J., J.U.D., The Pauline Privilege, XV-165 pp., 1931.
69. Donohue, Rev. John F., J.C.D., The Impediment of Crime, VII-110 pp., 1931.
70. Dooley, Rev. Eugene A., O.M.I., J.C.D., Church Law on Sacred Relics, IX-143 pp., 1931.
71. Orth, Rev. Clement Raymond, O.M.C., J.C.D., The Approbation of Religious Institutes, 171 pp., 1931.
72. Pernicone, Rev. Joseph M., A.B., J.C.D., The Ecclesiastical Prohibition of Books, XII-267 pp., 1932.
73. Clinton, Rev. Connell, A.B., J.C.D., The Paschal Precept, IX-108 pp., 1932.
74. Donnelly, Rev. Francis B., A.M., S.T.L., J.C.D., The Diocesan Synod, VIII-125 pp., 1932.
75. Torrente, Rev. Camilo, C.M.F., J.C.D., Las Procesiones Sagradas, V-145 pp., 1932.
76. Murphy, Rev. Edwin J., C.PP.S., J.C.D., Suspension Ex Informata Conscientia, XI-122 pp., 1932.
77. MacKenzie, Rev. Eric F., A.M., S.T.L., J.C.D., The Delict of Heresy in its Commission, Penalization, Absolution, VII-124 pp., 1932.
78. Lyons, Rev. Avitus E., S.T.B., J.C.D., The Collegiate Tribunal of First Instance, XI-147 pp., 1932.
79. Connolly, Rev. Thomas A., J.C.D., Appeals, XI-195 pp., 1932.
80. Sangmeister, Rev. Joseph V., A.B., J.C.D., Force and Fear as Precluding Matrimonial Consent, V-211 pp., 1932.
81. Jaeger, Rev. Leo A., A.B., J.C.D., The Administration of Vacant and Quasi-Vacant Episcopal Sees in the United States, IX-229 pp., 1932.
82. Rimlinger, Rev. Herbert T., J.C.D., Error Invalidating Matrimonial Consent, VII-79 pp., 1932.
83. Barrett, Rev. John D. M., S.S., J.C.D., A Comparative Study of the Third Plenary Council of Baltimore and the Code, IX-221 pp., 1932.
84. Carberry, Rev. John J., Ph.D., S.T.D., J.C.D., The Juridical Form of Marriage, X-177 pp., 1934.
85. Dolan, Rev. John L., A.B., J.C.D., The Defensor Vinculi, XII-157 pp., 1934.

86. HANNAN, REV. JEROME D., A.M., S.T.D., LL.B., J.C.D., The Canon Law of Wills, IX-517 pp., 1934.

87. LEMIEUX, REV. DELISE A., A.M., J.C.D., The Sentence in Ecclesiastical Procedure, IX-131 pp., 1934.

88. O'ROURKE, REV. JAMES J., A.B., J.C.D., Parish Registers, VII-109 pp., 1934.

89. TIMLIN, REV. BARTHOLOMEW, O.F.M., A.M., J.C.D., Conditional Matrimonial Consent, X-381 pp., 1934.

90. WAHL, REV. FRANCIS X., A.B., J.C.D., The Matrimonial Impediments of Consanguinity and Affinity, VI-125 pp., 1934.

91. WHITE, REV. ROBERT J., A.B., LL.B., S.T.B., J.C.D., Canonical Ante-Nuptial Promises and the Civil Law, VI-152 pp., 1934.

92. HERRERA, REV. ANTONIO PARRA, O.C.D., J.C.D., Legislacion Ecclesiastica sobra el Ayuno y la Abstinencia, XI-191 pp., 1935.

93. KENNEDY, REV. EDWIN J., J.C.D., The Special Matrimonial Process in Cases of Evident Nullity, X-165 pp., 1935.

94. MANNING, REV. JOHN J., A.B., J.C.D., Presumption of Law in Matrimonial Procedure, XI-111 pp., 1935.

95. MOEDER, REV. JOHN M., J.C.D., The Proper Bishop for Ordination and Dimissorial Letters, VII-135 pp., 1935.

96. O'MARA, REV. WILLIAM A., A.B., J.C.D., Canonical Causes for Matrimonial Dispensations, IX-155 pp., 1935.

97. REILLY, REV. PETER, J.C.D., Residence of Pastors, IX-81 pp., 1935.

98. SMITH, REV. MARINER T., O.P., S.T.Lr., J.C.D., The Penal Law for Religious, VII-169 pp., 1935.

99. WHALEN, REV. DONALD W., A.M., J.C.D., The Value of Testimonial Evidence in Matrimonial Procedure, XIII-297 pp., 1935.

100. CLEARY, REV. JOSEPH F., J.C.D., Canonical Limitations on the Alienation of Church Property, VIII-141 pp., 1936.

101. GLYNN, REV. JOHN C., J.C.D., The Promoter of Justice, XX-337 pp., 1936.

102. BRENNAN, REV. JAMES H., S.S., M.A., S.T.B., J.C.D., The Simple Convalidation of Marriage, VI-135 pp., 1937.

103. BRUNINI, REV. JOSEPH BERNARD, J.C.D., The Clerical Obligations of Canons 139 and 142, X-121 pp., 1937.

104. CONNOR, REV. MAURICE, A.B., J.C.D., The Administrative Removal of Pastors, VIII-159 pp., 1937.

105. GUILFOYLE, REV. MERLIN JOSEPH, J.C.D., Custom, XI-144 pp., 1937.

106. HUGHES, REV. JAMES AUSTIN, A.B., A.M., J.C.D., Witnesses in Criminal Trials of Clerics, IX-140 pp., 1937.

107. JANSEN, REV. RAYMOND J., A.B., S.T.L., J.C.D., Canonical Provisions for Catechetical Instruction, VII-153 pp., 1937.

108. KEALY, REV. JOHN JAMES, A.B., J.C.D., The Introductory Libellus in Church Court Procedure, XI-121 pp., 1937.

109. McMANUS, REV. JAMES EDWARD, C.SS.R., J.C.D., The Administration of Temporal Goods in Religious Institutes, XVI-196 pp., 1937.

110. MORIARTY, REV. EUGENE JAMES, J.C.D., Oaths in Ecclesiastical Courts, X-115 pp., 1937.

111. RAINER, REV. ELIGIUS GEORGE, C.SS.R., J.C.D., Suspension of Clerics, XVII-249 pp., 1937.

112. REILLY, REV. THOMAS F., C.SS.R., J.C.D., Visitation of Religious, VI-195 pp., 1938.

113. MORIARTY, REV. FRANCIS E. C.SS.R., J.C.D., The Extraordinary Absolution from Censures, XV-334 pp., 1938.

114. CONNOLLY, REV. NICHOLAS P., J.C.D., The Canonical Erection of Parishes, X-132 pp., 1938.

115. DONOVAN, REV. JAMES JOSEPH, J.C.D., The Pastor's Obligation in Prenuptial Investigation, XII-322 pp., 1938.

116. HARRIGAN, REV. ROBERT J., M.A., S.T.B., J.C.D., The Radical Sanation of Invalid Marriages, VIII-208 pp., 1938.

117. BOFFA, REV. CONRAD HUMBERT, J.C.D., Canonical Provisions for Catholic Schools, VII-211 pp., 1939.

118. PARSONS, REV. ANSCAR JOHN, O.M.Cap., J.C.D., Canonical Elections, XII-236 pp., 1939.

119. REILLY, REV. EDWARD MICHAEL, A.B., J.C.D., The General Norms of Dispensation, XII-156 pp., 1939.

120. RYAN, REV. GERALD ALOYSIUS, A.B., J.C.D., Principles of Episcopal Jurisdiction, XII-172 pp., 1939.

121. BURTON, REV. FRANCIS JAMES, C.S.C., A.B., J.C.D., A Commentary on Canon 1125, X-222 pp., 1940.

122. MIASKIEWICZ, REV. FRANCIS SIGISMUND, J.C.D., Supplied Jurisdiction According to Canon 209, XII-340 pp., 1940.

123. RICE, REV. PATRICK WILLIAM, A.B., J.C.D., Proof of Death in Prenuptial Investigation, VIII-156 pp., 1940.

124. ANGLIN, REV. THOMAS FRANCIS, M.S., J.C.D., The Eucharistic Fast, VIII-183 pp., 1941.

125. COLEMAN, REV. JOHN JEROME, J.C.D., The Minister of Confirmation, VI-153 pp., 1941.

126. DOWNS, REV. JOSEPH EMMANUEL, A.B., J.C.D., The Concept of Clerical Immunity, XI-163 pp., 1941.

127. ESSWEIN, REV. ANTHONY ALBERT, J.C.D., Extrajudicial Penal Powers of Ecclesiastical Superiors, X-144 pp., 1941.

128. FARRELL, REV. BENJAMIN FRANCIS, M.A., S.T.L., J.C.D., The Rights and Duties of the Local Ordinary Regarding Congregations of Women Religious of Pontifical Approval, V-195 pp., 1941.

129. FEENEY, REV. THOMAS JOHN, A.B., S.T.L., J.C.D., Restitutio in Integrum, VI-169 pp., 1941.

130. FINDLAY, REV. STEPHEN WILLIAM, O.S.B., A.B., J.C.D., Canonical

Norms Governing the Deposition and Degradation of Clerics, XVII-279 pp., 1941.

131. GOODWINE, REV. JOHN, A.B., S.T.L., J.C.D., The Right of the Church to Acquire Property, VIII-119 pp., 1941.

132. HESTON, REV. EDWARD LOUIS, C.S.C., Ph.D., S.T.D., J.C.D., The Alienation of Church Property in the United States, XII-222 pp., 1941.

133. HOGAN, REV. JAMES JOHN, A.B., S.T.L., J.C.D., Judicial Advocates and Procurators, XIII-200 pp., 1941.

134. KEALY, REV. THOMAS M., A.B., Litt.B., J.C.D., Dowry of Women Religious, IX-152 pp., 1941.

135. KEENE, REV. MICHAEL JAMES, O.S.B., J.C.D., Religious Ordinaries and Canon 198, V-164 pp., 1942.

136. KERIN, REV. CHARLES A., S.S., M.A., S.T.B., J.C.D., The Privation of Christian Burial, XVI-279 pp., 1941.

137. LOUIS, REV. WILLIAM FRANCIS, M.A., J.C.D., Diocesan Archives, X-101 pp., 1941.

138. McDEVITT, REV. GILBERT JOSEPH, A.B., J.C.D., Legitimacy and Legitimation, X-247 pp., 1941.

139. McDONOUGH, REV. THOMAS JOSEPH, A.B., J.C.D., Apostolic Administrators, X-217 pp., 1941.

140. **MEIER, REV. CARL ANTHONY, A.B., J.C.D., Penal Administrative Pro**cedure Against Negligent Pastors, XI-240 pp., 1941.

141. SCHMIDT, REV. JOHN ROGG, A.B., J.C.D., The Principles of Authentic Interpretation in Canon 17 of the Code of Canon Law, XII-331 pp., 1941.

142. SLAFKOSKY, REV. ANDREW LEONARD, A.B., J.C.D., The Canonical Episcopal Visitation of the Diocese, X-197 pp., 1941.

143. SWOBODA, REV. INNOCENT ROBERT, O.F.M., J.C.D., Ignorance in Relation to the Imputability of Delicts, IX-271 pp., 1941.

144. DUBÉ, REV. ARTHUR JOSEPH, A.B., J.C.D., The General Principles for the Reckoning of Time in Canon Law, VIII-299 pp., 1941.

145. McBRIDE, REV. JAMES T., A.B., J.C.D., Incardination and Excardination of Seculars, XX-585 pp., 1941.

146. KRÓL, REV. JOHN T., J.C.D., The Defendant in Contentious Trials, XII-207 pp., 1942.

147. COMYNS, REV. JOSEPH J., C.SS.R., A.B., J.C.D., Papal and Episcopal Administration of Church Property, XIV-155 pp., 1942.

148. BARRY, REV. GARRETT FRANCIS, O.M.I., J.C.D., Violation of the Cloister, XII-260 pp., 1942.

149. BOLDUC, REV. GATIEN, C.S.V., A.B., S.T.L., J.C.D., Les Études dans les Religions Cléricales, VIII-155 pp., 1942.

150. BOYLE, REV. DAVID JOHN, M.A., J.C.D., The Juridic Effects of Moral Certitude on Pre-Nuptial Guarantees, XII-188 pp., 1942.

151. **CANAVAN, REV. WALTER JOSEPH, M.A., Litt.D., J.C.D., The Profes**sion of Faith, XII-143 pp., 1942.

152. **Desrochers, Rev. Bruno, A.B., Ph.L., S.T.B., J.C.D., Le Premier Concile Plénier de Québec et le Code de Droit Canonique, XIV–186 pp., 1942.**

153. Dillon, Rev. Robert Edward, A.B., J.C.D., Common Law Marriage, X-148 pp., 1942.

154. **Dodwell, Rev. Edward John, Ph.D., S.T.B., J.C.D., The Time and** Place for the Celebration of Marriage, X-156 pp., 1942.

155. Donnellan, Rev. Thomas Andrew, A.B., J.C.D., The Obligation of the Missa pro Populo, VII-131 pp., 1942.

156. Eltz, Rev. Louis Anthony, A.B., J.C.D., Cooperation in Crime, XII-208 pp., 1942.

157. Gass, Rev. Sylvester Francis, M.A., J.C.D., Ecclesiastical Pensions, XI-206 pp., 1942.

158. Guiniven, Rev. John Joseph, C.SS.R., J.C.D., The Precept of Hearing Mass, XIV-188 pp., 1942.

159. Gulczynski, Rev. John Theophilus, J.C.D., The Desecration and Violation of Churches, X-126 pp., 1942.

160. Hammill, Rev. John Leo, M.A., J.C.D., The Obligations of the Traveler According to Canon 14, VIII-204 pp., 1942.

161. Haydt, Rev. John Joseph, A.B., J.C.D., Reserved Benefices, XI-148 pp., 1942.

162. Huser, Rev. Roger John, O.F.M., A.B., J.C.D., The Crime of Abortion in Canon Law, XII-187 pp., 1942.

163. **Kearney, Rev. Francis Patrick, A.B., S.T.L., J.C.D., The Principles of Canon 1127, X-162 pp., 1942.**

164. Linahen, Rev. Leo James, S.T.L., J.C.D., De Absolutione Complicis In Peccato Turpi, 114 pp., 1942.

165. McCloskey, Rev. Joseph Aloysius, A.B., J.C.D., The Subject of Ecclesiastical Law According to Canon 12, XVII-246 pp., 1942.

166. O'Neill, Rev. Francis Joseph, C.SS.R., J.C.D., The Dismissal of Religious in Temporary Vows, XIII-220 pp., 1942.

167. **Prince, Rev. John Edward, A.B., S.T.B., J.C.D., The Diocesan Chan**cellor, X-136 pp., 1942.

168. Riesner, Rev. Albert Joseph, C.SS.R., J.C.D., Apostates and Fugitives from Religious Institutes, IX-168 pp., 1942.

169. Stenger, Rev. Joseph Bernard, J.C.D., The Mortgaging of Church Property, 186 pp., 1942.

170. Waldron, Rev. Joseph Francis, A.B., J.C.D., The Minister of Baptism, XII-197 pp., 1942.

171. Willett, Rev. Robert Albert, J.C.D., The Probative Value of Documents in Ecclesiastical Trials, X-124 pp., 1942.

172. Woeber, Rev. Edward Martin, M.A., J.C.D., The Interpellations, XII-161 pp., 1942.

173. Benko, Rev. Matthew Aloysius, O.S.B., M.A., J.C.D., The Abbot *Nullius*, XIV-148 pp., 1943.

174. CHRIST, REV. JOSEPH JAMES, M.A., S.T.L., J.C.D., Dispensation from Vindicative Penalties, XIV-285 pp., 1943.

175. CLANCY, REV. PATRICK M. J., O.P., A.B., S.T.Lr., J.C.D., The Local Religious Superior, X-229 pp., 1943.

176. CLARKE, REV. THOMAS JAMES, J.C.D., Parish Societies, XII-147 pp., 1943.

177. CONNOLLY, REV. JOHN PATRICK, S.T.L., J.C.D., Synodal Examiners and Parish Priest Consultors, X-223 pp., 1943.

178. DRUMM, REV. WILLIAM MARTIN, A.B., J.C.D., Hospital Chaplains, XII-175 pp., 1943.

179. FLANAGAN, REV. BERNARD JOSEPH, A.B., S.T.L., J.C.D., The Canonical Erection of Religious Houses, X-147 pp., 1943.

180. KELLEHER, REV. STEPHEN JOSEPH, A.B., S.T.B., J.C.D., Discussions with Non-Catholics: Canonical Legislation, X-93 pp., 1943.

181. LEWIS, REV. GORDIAN, C.P., J.C.D., Chapters in Religious Institutes, XII-169 pp., 1943.

182. MARX, REV. ADOLPH, J.C.D., The Declaration of Nullity of Marriages Contracted Outside the Church, X-151 pp., 1943.

183. MATULENAS, REV. RAYMOND ANTHONY, O.S.B., A.B., J.C.D., Communication, a Source of Privileges, XII-225 pp., 1943.

184. O'LEARY, REV. CHARLES GERARD, C.SS.R., J.C.D., Religious Dismissed After Perpetual Profession, X-213 pp., 1943.

185. POWER, REV. CORNELIUS MICHAEL, J.C.D., The Blessing of Cemeteries, XII-231 pp., 1943.

186. SHUHLER, REV. RALPH VINCENT, O.S.A., J.C.D., Privileges of Regulars to Absolve and Dispense, XII-195 pp., 1943.

187. ZIOLKOWSKI, REV. THADDEUS STANISLAUS, A.B., J.C.D., The Consecration and Blessing of Churches, XII-151 pp., 1943.

188. HENEGHAN, REV. JOHN JOSEPH, S.T.D., J.C.D., The Marriages of Unworthy Catholics: Canons 1065 and 1066, XVI-213 pp., 1944.

189. CARROLL, REV. COLEMAN FRANCIS, M.A., S.T.L., J.C.L., Charitable Institutions.

190. CIESLUK, REV. JOSEPH EDWARD, Ph.B., S.T.L., J.C.L., National Parishes in the United States.

191. COBURN, REV. VINCENT PAUL, A.B., J.C.D., Marriages of Conscience, XII-172 pp., 1944.

192. CONNORS, REV. CHARLES PAUL, C.S.Sp., A.B., J.C.D., Extra-Judicial Procurators in the Code of Canon Law, X-94 pp., 1944.

193. COYLE, REV. PAUL RAYMOND, A.B., J.C.D., Judicial Exceptions, X-142 pp., 1944.

194. FAIR, REV. BARTHOLOMEW FRANCIS, A.B., S.T.L., J.C.D., The Impediment of Abduction.

195. GALLAGHER, REV. THOMAS RAPHAEL, O.P., A.B., S.T.Lr., J.C.D., The Examination of the Qualities of the Ordinand, X-166 pp., 1944.

196. GANNON, REV. JOHN MARK, S.T.L., J.C.D., The Interstices Required for the Promotion to Orders, XII-100 pp., 1944.

197. GOLDSMITH, REV. J. WILLIAM, B.C.S., S.T.L., J.C.D., The Competence of Church and State over Marriage—Disputed Points, X-128 pp., 1944.

198. GOODWINE, REV. JOSEPH GERARD, A.B., S.T.B., J.C.D., The Receptioı of Converts, XIV-326 pp., 1944.

199. KOWALSKI, REV. ROMUALD EUGENE, O.F.M., A.B., J.C.D., Sustenance of Religious Houses of Regulars, X-174 pp., 1944.

200. McCOY, REV. ALAN EDWARD, O.F.M., J.C.D., Force and Fear in Relation to Delictual Imputability and Penal Responsibility, XII-160 pp., 1944.

201. McDEVITT, REV. VINCENT JOHN, Ph.B., S.T.L., J.C.L., Perjury.

202. MARTIN, REV. THOMAS OWEN, Ph.D., S.T.D., J.C.D., Adverse Possession, Prescription and Limitation of Actions: The Canonical "Praescriptio," XX-208 pp., 1944.

203. MIKLOSOVIC, REV. PAUL JOHN, A.B., J.C.L., Attempted Marriages and Their Consequent Juridic Effects.

204. MUNDY, REV. THOMAS MAURICE, A.B., S.T.L., J.C.D., The Union of Parishes, X—164 pp., 1945.

205. O'DEA, REV. JOHN COYLE, A.B., J.C.D., The Matrimonial Impediment of Nonage, VIII-126 pp., 1944.

206. OLALIA, REV. ALEXANDER AYSON, S.T.L., J.C.D., A Comparative Study of the Christian Constitution of States and the Constitution of the **Philippine Commonwealth, XII—136 pp., 1944.**

207. POISSON, REV. PIERRE-MARIE, C.S.C., A.B., Ph.L., Th.L., J.C.L., Droits Patrimoniaux des Maisons et des Églises Religieuses.

208. STADALNIKAS, REV. CASIMIR JOSEPH, M.I.C., J.C.D., Reservation of Censures, X-141 pp., 1944.

209. SULLIVAN, REV. EUGENE HENRY, S.T.L., J.C.D., Proof of the Reception of the Sacraments, X—165 pp., 1944.

210. VAUGHAN, REV. WILLIAM EDWARD, J.C.D., Constitutions for Diocesan Courts, X-210 pp., 1944.

211. PARO, REV. GINO, S.T.D., J.C.L., The Right of Apostolic Legation.

212. BALZER, REV. RALPH FRANCIS, C.P., J.C.D., The Computation of Time in a Canonical Novitiate.

213. DOUGHERTY, REV. JOHN WHELAN, A.B., S.T.L., J.C.D., De Inquisitione Speciali.

214. DZIOB, REV. MICHAEL WALTER, J.C.D., The Sacred Congregation for the Oriental Church.

215. EIDENSCHINK, REV. JOHN ALBERT, O.S.B., B.A., J.C.D, The Election of Bishops in the Letters of Pope Gregory the Great.

216. GILL, REV. NICHOLAS, C.P., J.C.D., The Spiritual Prefect in Clerical

217. HYNES, REV. HARRY GERARD, S.T.L., J.C.D., The Privileges of Cardinals, XII-183 pp., 1945.

218. McDEVITT, REV. GERALD VINCENT, S.T.L., J.C.D., The Renunciation of an Ecclesiastical Office, XIV—179 pp., 1946.

219. MANNING, REV. JOSEPH LEROY, J.C.D., The Free Conferral of Offices.
220. MEYER, REV. LOUIS G., O.S.B., A.B., S.T.B., J.C.D., Alms-Gathering by Religious, XII—163 pp., 1946.
221. O'DONNELL, REV. CLETUS FRANCIS, M.A., J.C.L., The Marriage of Minors.
222. PRUNSKIS, REV. JOSEPH, J.C.D., Comparative Law, Ecclesiastical and Civil, in Lithuanian Concordat, X—161 pp., 1945.
223. SWEENEY, REV. FRANCIS PATRICK, C.SS.R., J.C.D., The Reduction of Clerics to the Lay State, X—199 pp., 1945.
224. VOGELPOHL, REV. HENRY JOHN, J.C.D., The Simple Impediments to Holy Orders.
225. BROCKHAUS, REV. THOMAS AQUINAS, O.S.B., A.B., J.C.D., Religious who Are Known as *Conversi.*
226. GRIESE, REV. N. ORVILLE, S.T.D., J.C.D., The Marriage Contract and the Procreation of Offspring, XVI-224 pp., 1946.
227. BOUDREAUX, REV. WARREN LOUIS, J.C.L., The "*ab acatholicis nati*" of Canon 1099, § 2.
228. BOWE, REV. THOMAS JOSEPH, A.B., J.C.D., Religious Superioresses, VIII-206 pp., 1946.
229. DIEDERICHS, REV. MICHAEL FERDINAND, S.C.J., J.C.D., The Jurisdiction of the Latin Ordinaries over their Oriental Subjects, XIV-153 pp., 1946.
230. DINGMAN, REV. MAURICE JOHN, A.B., S.T.L., J.C.L., The Plaintiff in Contentious Trials.
231. FRISON, REV. BASIL, C.M.F., M.MUS., J.C.D., The Retroactivity of Law, X-221 pp., 1946.
232. GALVIN, REV. WILLIAM ANTHONY, M.A., J.C.D., The Administrative Transfer of Pastors, XII-288 pp., 1946.
233. GORACY, REV. JOSEPH C., J.C.L., The Diriment Matrimonial Impediment of Major Orders.
234. HALE, REV. JOSEPH FRANCIS, M.A., S.T.L., J.C.L., The Pastor of Burial.
235. HENRY, REV. JOSEPH ARTHUR, A.B., J.C.D., The Mass and Holy Communion: Inter-Ritual Law, XII-138 pp., 1946.
236. LINENBERGER, REV. HERBERT, C.PP.S., J.C.L., The False Denunciation of an Innocent Confessor.
237. LOWRY, REV. JAMES MARTIN, A.B., J.C.D., Dispensation from Private Vows, XII-266 pp., 1946.
238. LYNCH, REV. GEORGE EDWARD, A.B., S.T.L., J.C.D., Coadjutors and Auxiliaries of Bishops, X-107 pp., 1947.
239. LYNCH, REV. TIMOTHY, M.S.SS.T., J.C.D., Contracts between Bishops and Religious Congregations, XIV-232 pp., 1946.
240. McCLUNN, REV. JUSTIN DAVID, A.B., S.T.L., J.C.D., Administrative Recourse, VII-142 pp., 1946.

241. Lohmuller, Rev. Martin Nicholas, A.B., J.C.D., The Promulgation of Law, XII-140 pp., 1947.
242. McGrath, Rev. James, A.B., J.C.D., The Privilege of the Canon, XII-156 pp., 1946.
243. Marbach, Rev. Joseph Francis, A.B., J.C.D., Marriage Legislation for the Catholics of the Oriental Rites in the United States and Canada, XIV-314 pp., 1946.
244. Shimkus, Rev. Bernard Aloyius, A.B., J.C.L., The Determination and Transfer of Rite.
245. Smith, Rev. Vincent Michael, A.B., S.T.L., J.C.L., Ignorance Affecting Matrimonial Consent.
246. Wachtrle, Rev. Paul Anthony, A.B., J.C.L., The Baptism of the Children of Non-Catholics.
247. Crotty, Rev. Matthew Michael, J.C.L., The Recipient of First Holy Communion.
248. Eagleton, Rev. George, J.C.L., The Quinquennial Faculties, Formula IV.
249. Gibbons, Rev. Marion Leo, C.M., J.C.L., Domicile of the Wife Unlawfully Separated from Her Husband.
250. Kelly, Rev. Bernard Matthew, J.C.L., The Functions Reserved to Pastors.
251. Kilcullen, Rev. Thomas John, J.C.L., The Collegiate Moral Person as Party Litigant.
252. Lafontaine, Rev. Germain Joseph, W.F., J.C.L., Relations Canoniques entre le Missionaire et Ses Superieurs.
253. Lane, Rev. Loras Thomas, J.C.L., Matrimonial Procedure in Ordinary Court of Second Instance.
254. Lover, Rev. James Francis, C.Ss.R., J.C.L., The Master of Novices.
255. McNicholas, Rev. Timothy Joseph, J.C.L., The *Septimae Manus* Witness.
256. Marositz, Rev. Joseph John, M.S.C., J.C.L., Obligations and Privileges of Religious Promoted to the Episcopal or Cardinalitial Dignities.
257. Murphy, Rev. Francis Joseph, J.C.L., Legislative Powers of the Provincial Council.
258. O'Brien, Rev. Romaeus William, O.Carm., J.C.L., The Provincial Superior in Religious Orders of Men.
259. Pfaller, Rev. Benedict Augustine, O.S.B., J.C.L., The *ipso facto* Effected Dismissal of Religious.
260. Popek, Rev. Alphonse Sylvester, J.C.L., The Rights and Obligations of Metropolitans.
261. Ristuccia, Rev. Bernard Joseph, C.M., J.C.L., Quasi-Religious.
262. Sonntag, Rev. Nathaniel Louis, O.F.M.Cap., J.C.L., Censorship of Special Classes of Books.
263. Stadler, Rev. Joseph Nicholas, J.C.L., Frequent Holy Communion.

264. SZAL, REV. IGNATIUS JOSEPH, J.C.L., The Communication of Catholics with Schismatics.
265. WAGNER, REV. URBAN STANLEY, O.F.M.Conv., J.C.L., Parochial Substitute Vicars and Supplying Priests.

www.ingramcontent.com/pod-product-compliance
Lightning Source LLC
LaVergne TN
LVHW050215080826
844660LV00012B/415
* 9 7 8 0 8 1 3 2 2 4 2 8 2 *